ANCIENT CULTURE AND SOCIETY

THE COMIC THEATRE OF
GREECE AND ROME

ANCIENT CULTURE AND SOCIETY

General Editor
M. I. FINLEY
*Master of Darwin College and
Professor of Ancient History
in the University of Cambridge*

A. W. H. ADKINS   Moral Values and Political
Behaviour in Ancient Greece
H. C. BALDRY   The Greek Tragic Theatre
P. A. BRUNT   Social Conflicts in the Roman Republic
M. I. FINLEY   Early Greece: the Bronze and Archaic Ages
Y. GARLAN   War in the Ancient World: A Social History
A. H. M. JONES   Augustus
G. E. R. LLOYD   Early Greek Science: Thales to Aristotle
G. E. R. LLOYD   Greek Science After Aristotle
C. MOSSÉ   The Ancient World at Work
R. M. OGILVIE   The Romans and Their Gods
F. H. SANDBACH   The Stoics
B. H. WARMINGTON   Nero: Reality and Legend

THE
COMIC THEATRE
OF GREECE AND
ROME

F. H. SANDBACH

Emeritus Professor of Classics
in the University of Cambridge

1977
CHATTO & WINDUS
LONDON

Published by
Chatto & Windus Ltd
40 William IV Street
London WC2N 4DF

*

Clarke, Irwin & Co. Ltd
Toronto

ISBN 0 7011 2193 9 (Hardback)
ISBN 0 7011 2194 7 (Paperback)

© F. H. Sandbach 1977

Printed in Great Britain by
Cox & Wyman Ltd
London, Fakenham and Reading

CONTENTS

FIGURES

PLATES

Plate 1a is reproduced by permission of The Metropolitan Museum of Art, New York; Plate 1b by permission of the American School of Classical Studies in Athens; Plate 2 by permission of the Vatican Museum; Plate 3 by permission of the Societies for the Promotion of Hellenic and Roman Studies and the Moretti Collection, Milan; Plate 4 by permission of The British Museum.

Preface

THE prime object of this book is not simply to evaluate the comedies that survive from the ancient world, but to explain what sort of plays were written and why they were written, how and where they were produced, and how they were related to the world in which they were performed.

Information about the conditions of drama, whether it is to be gathered from the authors of antiquity or from archaeological evidence, is patchy and often uncertain. Experts disagree about the inferences that can be drawn, not least on how to interpret the remains of ancient theatres. To avoid overburdening my text with the word 'probably', I have at times been more dogmatic than is fully justified, but hope that uncertainty over important issues has not been concealed.

Transliteration of Greek names is always a problem, and no doubt inconsistencies remain. My aim has been to anglicise or latinise those of historical personages and places, that being their most familiar form, but to retain Greek spelling for characters in and titles of plays, except for three by Aristophanes which have long had a latinised termination.

Drafts have been read by Dr Colin Austin, Mr Michael Meyer, and Professor Moses Finley, to all of whom I am greatly indebted for corrections, information, and suggestions. For errors which remain I alone am responsible.

F.H.S.

Introduction

THE names are known of nearly 250 authors of Greek comedy, dating from the sixth century BC to the second century AD. At the end of that century Athenaeus, a learned man with access to the great library of Alexandria at the mouth of the Nile, claimed to have read 800 comedies which had been composed in a period roughly corresponding to the years 400–325 BC. How much of all this vast and continuing production, testimony to the place of comedy in Greek civilisation, still survives today?

The plays of just one author of comedies were copied and read by the scholars of the later Byzantine Empire, to whom the preservation of classical Greek literature is owed. He was Aristophanes, whose power and versatility won him fame in Athens at the end of the fifth century BC, that period of astonishing creativity, literary, artistic and philosophical, the time of Euripides and Pheidias, Thucydides and Socrates; he had then worked on in the drabber years of the early fourth century when comedy set out on a road of development to a new form. Eleven of his comedies were all that these scholars found remaining out of a total of at least forty. But copies of them were taken to Italy, and so when Byzantium fell to the Turks in 1453 these eleven plays were not in danger of being lost to the world.

From the others, which had disappeared during the Dark Ages of the seventh and eighth centuries, when pagan literature was suspect, hated, neglected and destroyed, nothing was preserved but odd words, lines and short passages, few of more than eight or nine verses; these had been quoted by other authors whose works for some reason survived, particularly by grammarians and lexicon-makers who were interested in his copious vocabulary, much of which was by their time obsolete. Similar flotsam from the works of about 120 other comic authors survived in the same way. Some of

9

these comedians attracted the attention of anthologists in search of moral maxims and well-turned sentiments, while Athenaeus fished widely in their waters for passages connected with food, drink, cooks and dinner-parties.

The material gathered from such sources and first assembled in a publication of 1839–41 unavoidably gave a distorted picture of these lost dramas. But there is other evidence which could do something to correct it. Twenty plays by Plautus and six by Terence, Latin dramatists of the second century BC, are adaptations of Greek comedies, most of which indubitably belonged to the period 325–250. These Latin versions survive because some manuscripts written in the fourth or fifth centuries AD, when there were still educated laymen to read them, were kept and copied in medieval monasteries. From them a very good idea can be formed of the plots at any rate of the originals.

But until the twentieth century direct knowledge of Greek comedy was, with trifling exceptions, confined to what had been transmitted through the Byzantines. Now, however, a new source was found. Books in the ancient world were mostly written on papyrus, a material made from a reed which grows in Egypt. It was less durable than good modern paper, but it can survive well in very dry conditions, such as are provided by the rubbish-heaps and collapsed houses of parts of that country, which had come to have a partly hellenised population after its conquest by Alexander the Great. The possible rewards of excavating on suitable sites became apparent a hundred years ago, and a great deal of material was collected, mainly between 1895 and 1914.

Among this material many scraps have turned up from numerous different manuscripts which contained comedies, attesting the popularity of this form of literature among the inhabitants of these small Egyptian towns. The majority are from the works of Menander, (342–292), whose name was in antiquity coupled by some critics with that of Homer. More important, however, was the find in 1905 of nineteen leaves (some damaged) and other fragments of a manuscript which made it possible to form a picture of three of his plays. A still greater discovery came to light in 1958, when the existence was first reported of a manuscript which has proved to contain three plays by Menander; one is complete, while far the greater part of the second and more than half of the third are intact. Several other extensive texts also have been published since 1965. This new evidence has greatly extended understanding of his work and at the same time provided a wider and sounder basis for estimating the originality of the Latin dramatists.

In Greece public performances of drama were usually part of a religious festival, included in the official proceedings. The arrangements were in the hands of the authorities responsible for the festival. It was also usual that plays should be presented in competition with one another and that prizes should be awarded to those judged to be the best.

Drama was not necessarily an original feature of the festivals at which it was performed. No doubt it was immediately part of the programme at some festivals that were comparatively late institutions, like those established at many places during the century that followed the death of Alexander the Great. But at Athens, although comedy was presented at festivals of great antiquity, it was not taken under official patronage before the fifth century BC; this step was taken as late as about 440 at the Lenaia, where it always overshadowed tragedy, whereas the City Dionysia, where it was subordinate, included it as early as 486. To recapture the religious feelings of past civilisations may be impossible, but perhaps these old Athenians thought that their god Dionysus would share their pleasure in dramatic performances.

Competition was dear to the Greeks. The athletic contests at the court of Alcinous in the *Odyssey* appear to be purely secular, but the four great religious panhellenic festivals at Olympia, Delphi, Nemea and the Isthmus of Corinth, centred on a variety of races and other contests; at Delphi athletic events were an addition to original musical competitions for pipers, lyre-players and singers who accompanied themselves on the lyre. At Athens a torch-race was held at more than one festival, and after Peisistratus' expansion of the Panathenaia in the sixth century prizes were offered there for the recital of Homer and for performances with pipe and lyre as well as for athletics and horse-racing. Consequently it is not surprising that when drama became part of two Dionysiac festivals, it too was made the occasion for competition.

The festival of the Lenaia was so-called after the *lēnai*, a name for ecstatic women experiencing possession by the god Dionysus. There is no evidence to show that they still played a part in its celebration in the fifth century. All that is certain is that there was a procession and, after 440, dramatic contests. Procession and plays were under the care of the 'king', one of the nine annual magistrates, the residual heir of a former monarchy. To him dramatists who wished to have their plays performed 'applied for a chorus', and he allotted choruses for two tragedies and five comedies. It is not known on what grounds he exercised his choice; poets certainly had not completed their plays at this point; occasionally two plays by the same author were selected. The duty of providing the choruses fell upon well-to-do citizens, one for each play, who became its *chorēgos*, literally 'chorus-leader', although he took no part in the actual performance; his task was to recruit its members, able to sing and to dance, provide their costumes, and pay a trainer and a piper who accompanied their songs. This was one of the 'liturgies', or public services, required of the wealthier citizens, whom civic and personal pride often forbade to stint their expenditure; it was easy to lay out fifteen minae on a comedy, the price of ten able-bodied slaves, even although the 'king' was responsible for hiring and paying the leading actor from public funds; he in his turn may have engaged the rest of the cast.

Arrangements were much the same at the City Dionysia, the other Athenian festival at which plays were presented. But the magistrate in charge was the *archōn epōnymos*, not the 'king'; he too was annually appointed and given his title because his name was used in the Athenian calendar to identify the year in which he held office. In contrast with the Lenaia, tragedy here had first place, occupying the theatre for three days, on each of which were performed three tragedies and a satyr-play. An earlier day may have seen five comedies[1] and before

---

[1] It is orthodox to suppose that during the Peloponnesian War the number of comedies was reduced for reasons of economy to

that at least a day must have been given to dithyrambs, songs in honour of gods, sung by choirs of fifty; each of the ten 'tribes', into which the citizens were divided, provided two choirs, one of men and one of boys.

These singers of dithyrambs cannot have been professionals, and it is a striking fact that such a large number of citizens were actively engaged as competitors at this festival. The chorusmen of tragedy and comedy were also citizens and there is nothing to show that in the fifth century they received any pay, apart from some possible 'fringe benefits'. We should probably see most of them as what we should call 'experienced amateurs'.

Every dramatist whose work was performed received a payment; it is not known whether the winner had any reward beyond a garland of ivy; there is a little evidence to show that second and third were also places of honour, as they are in modern athletic events. Not only were the poets in competition, but often the leading actors also; at the Lenaia a prize for the best comic actor seems to have been instituted at the same time as comedy, but there was none at the City Dionysia until some date between 329 and 312, although tragic actors had competed there from about 450. The successful actor did not by any means always appear in the winning play. It may be added that there is no record at any time, whether in literature or in inscriptions, of any man who acted both in tragedy and in comedy on the Greek stage. Nor were dramatists active in both fields; when Socrates at the end of Plato's *Symposium* forces the tragic poet Agathon and Aristophanes the comedian to admit that it is the same man who can write tragedy and comedy, that was an outrageous paradox.

---

three, and that one was performed after each satyr-play. A strong case against this has been made by W. Luppe, *Philologus* 116 (1972) pp. 53–75. We do not know that the comedies normally came between the dithyrambs and the tragedies, but official records always give the winners in the order boys' dithyramb, men's dithyramb, comedy, tragedy.

An Athenian Comedy

To say that we possess eleven plays by Aristophanes, the Athenian writer of comedies, is a half-truth. We have the words of eleven plays. But the text is not the play. The play was a single performance in the theatre at Athens, spoken and acted by costumed actors and in part sung by a chorus of dancers to the music of a piper. There is no record that any of the eleven plays was performed more than once except *Frogs* of 405 B C, and that was mentioned because it was exceptional. The experience of that original audience cannot be recaptured; the melodies they heard are lost for ever, and many of the jokes need explanation, which may give understanding, but does not encourage laughter. Yet imagination can do something to reconstruct the scene and, aided by information and hints to be found in ancient authors, do much to revivify the words. The stage can be before the mind's eye and the actors seen to move upon it; although these ghostly figures can do little to re-create that rapport with the audience and elicit that response from it without which a play is a failure, although the infectious laughter of the spectators is now silent and the topical allusions stir no emotions, the attempt must be made to transport ourselves back from the isolated chair in our house or library to a seat on a crowded Athenian hillside.

The year is 425 B C. It is midwinter, although the days have begun to lengthen. The festival of the Lenaia has returned to cheer the people. The Peloponnesian War has been in progress for more than five years, and farms have suffered the ravages of annual invasions; crops have been destroyed, here and there vines slashed, olives cut down, houses burnt. Every year the country population has been obliged to take refuge behind the walls which connect the city with its port, the Peiraeus. But command of the sea secures Athenian property in the Aegean islands, widespread trade, and tribute from the subject 'allies'.

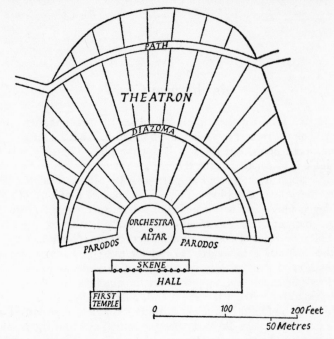

FIG. 1 *Sketch-plan of Theatre of Dionysus in the time of Aristophanes*

Let us go with the crowds at daybreak to the theatre (see Fig. 1), not forgetting a cushion and some food, for the performances will proceed without pause for the whole day. The auditorium has been formed in a hollow on the south side of the Acropolis; it is possible to reach the higher tiers by a path part way up, but we will enter at the lowest level by one of the *parodoi* or ways-in, which lead past the ends of the roughly semi-circular rows of wooden seating, and then climb up by one of the sets of steeply rising steps which intersect them. From our seats we look down on a circular area of hard-trodden earth, across which we have come; this is the *orchēstra*, or dancing-floor, about 22 yards in diameter, the length of a cricket-pitch, with an altar for Dionysus in the centre. Touching (or is it overlapping?) the far side runs a low platform; we can but guess its dimensions, perhaps 25 feet wide and 9

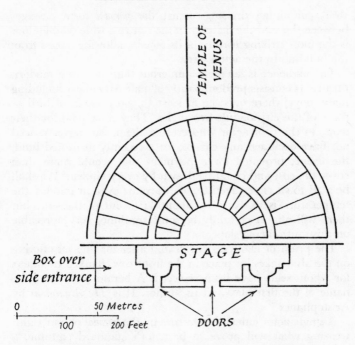

FIG. 2 *Sketch-plan of Pompey's Theatre at Rome*

feet deep.[1] A few steps connect this platform with the orchestra; we shall be interested to see whether they form a kind of short stairway or run all the way round. Behind and extending to the sides far beyond it is a building of thick timbers, the

[1] The description of the theatre depends on archaeological evidence difficult to interpret and much disputed. My text gives what I think to be a very probable account that is widely but not unanimously held. There are even those who argue that the performances at the Lenaia, unlike those at the City Dionysia (see p. 26), were not given in the theatre at all. This is typical of the problems which face the historian of ancient drama. The earlier writers of antiquity often fail to record what they suppose everyone must know, while later ones may be suspected of knowing no more than we do and of resorting, like us, to guesswork.

17

skēnē, containing dressing-rooms; the *parodoi* form passages between this and the seating. In the centre a wide double-door is the most striking feature of its façade, allowing access from the building to the acting area.

The audience is far more numerous than that of a modern theatre. It consists predominantly of male Athenians, including many boys; there must be at least 15,000 present, a third or more of the city's adult free males. They have paid for their seats, to the contractor who erected them. But poverty need not have excluded any citizen, for a recently instituted fund, the *theōric*, provided for a payment that would more than cover the cost and could be drawn by every citizen.[1] We shall be glad to sit close together, for warmth; even at midday the temperature is likely to be about 11 °C out of the sun; but there will almost certainly be some sunshine, very agreeable on this south-facing slope.

The priest of Dionysus enters and after making an offering on the altar takes his place in the front row, flanked by others for whom seats have been reserved. A herald announces the name of the first play and its author. It is *The Acharnians* by Aristophanes.[2]

A single actor enters the *orchestra* by the *parodos* on our right, wearing what will prove to be actor's standard costume, a mask that covers the whole face and flesh-coloured tights that reach to the wrists and ankles, with padded belly and buttocks; to these tights is attached an exaggerated phallus, revealed by an unnaturally short tunic. From his words, spoken in verse, as all the play will be, it soon appears that he is to be thought of as in the Pnyx, the open space on a low hill where there was held, at least three times a month, a general assembly of the Athenian people. He begins with some jokes at the expense

[1] This is a probability only. Theoric payments are explicitly attested only for the City Dionysia, the other festival at which there were dramatic performances.

[2] This is an arbitrary assumption. The play was presented at the Lenaia of 425, but its place in the programme is not known. Moreover, although its text assumes the audience to be aware that Aristophanes is the author, the producer was, as for his two earlier plays, his friend Callistratus; he and not Aristophanes may have been named by the herald.

of the politician Cleon, of Theognis, a writer of tragedies, of two singers and a piper, then complains of the dilatoriness of the people to attend the meeting; even its officers come pushing in at the last moment and never give a thought to making peace. He himself is always the first to arrive and sits there 'groaning, yawning, stretching, farting, puzzling, doodling, pulling out hairs and doing sums, looking towards his farm, longing for peace'. Today he has come prepared to create a scene unless peace is discussed.

Suddenly the assembly is filling; a herald calls for speakers. The first is Amphitheos, who presents himself as the goddess Demeter's grandson and complains that, although an immortal, he has been refused a grant of travelling-expenses to go to Sparta, where he proposes to conclude peace. In spite of protests by Dikaiopolis—that proves later to be the name of the character who had first appeared on the stage—he is seized by the police, who in Athens were slaves from Scythia. Next come ambassadors back from a visit to the King of Persia; they complain of their hardships, paid a mere two drachmas a day (four times a normal rate), forced to drink their wine neat out of golden cups, and fed on whole roast oxen. Dikaiopolis annotates their story with indecent comments. An ambassador then introduces Pseudartabas; in Greek the first part of this Persian-sounding name means 'false'. His mask has a huge eye, and he is alleged to be the official known as 'The King's Eye'. He speaks two lines; the first is gibberish, interpreted by the ambassador as promise of a subsidy; the second is broken Greek: 'no get money.' Dikaiopolis intervenes: 'Tell me, or I'll beat you black and blue, will the King send us money?'. The Eye indicates a negative. 'Then the ambassadors are fooling us?' Two 'eunuchs', who accompany the Eye, nod, so giving themselves away as Greeks. Dikaiopolis recognises them as two notorious supposed catamites, often ridiculed in comedies. The herald then announces that the Council invite the Eye to dinner, and Dikaiopolis gives Amphitheos eight drachmas to go to Sparta and bring back a private peace for him and his family.

The herald calls on an envoy who has been to the Thracian chief Sitalces. He introduces a troop of Thracian savages to be enlisted as mercenaries. They pounce upon Dikaiopolis, to steal and devour the garlic he has brought to go with his lunch. Protesting against this and crying that he has felt a drop of rain, he causes the assembly to be suspended. Amphitheos rushes in, saying that he is being pursued by the men of Acharnae, a large village north of the city, because he is bringing *spondai* from Sparta, literally wine for libation, but also a word for a treaty of peace. Dikaiopolis tastes three varieties, chooses that with the longest validity and by going through a door into the stage-building, enters his farmhouse, now suddenly represented by the stage-building; he has the intention of celebrating the country Dionysia. Amphitheos makes off by the *parodos* opposite that by which he had entered.

No sooner has he gone than the Acharnians, who form the chorus of this play, surge into the *orchestra*, twenty-four of them, dressed in masks and tights, tunics and cloaks, intent on lynching the traitor; but they draw aside at the appearance of a religious procession—such as had a place at the rural Dionysia—formed by Dikaiopolis and his daughter, who bears the sacred basket, and a slave carrying high and erect the emblematic phallus. Dikaiopolis sings of his joy at returning to his village and the even greater pleasure of having his way with a slave-girl caught stealing his wood. The Acharnians rush at him; his daughter and the slave must run in.

The metre changes: the lines are now not iambic trimeters but mostly long trochaics with some cretics and a few anapaests.[1] The exchanges between Dikaiopolis and the chorus or its leader are for sixty-two verses almost exactly balanced, and they may have been spoken to the music of a long-robed piper who has come in with the chorus. He has twin pipes, supported and held to his mouth by a band which passes round the back of his head. Dikaiopolis saves the situation by running into his house and coming out with a bag of charcoal as a hostage. Many Acharnians were charcoal burners and his device parodies Euripides' *Tēlephus*, produced thirteen years earlier, in which the hostage was a child. They are forced to allow him to put his case, which he proposes to do with his head upon a block; Telephus had said that even if his neck

[1] For these metrical terms see Glossary, p. 157.

were threatened by an axe, he would not keep silent. Dikaio-polis turns this figure of speech into a literal realisation.

The actor now turns to the audience and, reverting to iambic trimeters, reminds them how Cleon had dragged him before the Council on account of last year's comedy, perhaps a hint not to show such an absurd touchiness if they do not like what they are about to hear. For the moment he has taken on the person of the author. Then, making fun of a common practice of defendants in a court of law, he says that he must dress himself to look as wretched as possible; for this he will go to Euripides, who was notorious for introducing into his tragedies ragged heroes down on their luck. The central door now represents Euripides' house: a servant answers 'he is at home not at home'. Dikaiopolis persists and the poet, inter-rupted in composing a drama, consents to be wheeled out on the *ekkyklēma*, a device by which in tragedies a platform was pushed through the stage-door to reveal an interior tableau. In tragic language he grants requests made one by one for properties from his plays, until finally he exclaims: 'There all my plays are gone!' But his tormentor has not finished: 'I've forgotten the one thing on which everything depends. Sweetest and dearest little Euripides, may I be damned if I ask you for anything more, except one single thing, just this one thing, this one thing: let me have some chervil you got from your mother.'[1]

Dressed as a beggar, Dikaiopolis lays his head on the block and puts his case. He hates the Spartans, but this is a war about trifles. There had been an import ban, he says, on goods from Megara and a prostitute kidnapped from that town; the Megarians had retaliated by stealing two prostitutes from the establishment of Aspasia, Pericles' mistress. Thereupon Pericles carried a measure to outlaw Megarians by land and sea; the Spartans had then come to the aid of their allies, just as the Athenians would have rushed to arms to defend the least of *their* allies.

This speech divides the Acharnians. Those who are still indignant summon Lamachus, a popular general, who enters

---

[1] Aristophanes was fond of alleging that Euripides' mother had once sold vegetables on the market.

in battle array. Dikaiopolis simulates terror, but then accuses him of making a good thing out of war, unlike the honest men who serve in the ranks. 'O Democracy! can we stand this?' cries Lamachus and departs, declaring that he will always fight the Spartans everywhere. Dikaiopolis goes into his own house.

What follows brings a surprise. The Acharnians announce that they have been won over, but that they must strip for their anapaests. Dropping their cloaks, they advance towards us, the spectators, and their leader delivers a long speech in anapaestic metre:

> Never before, since he had charge of a comic chorus, has our author come forward to the spectators to tell them how clever he is. But now, being slandered by his enemies among the Athenians, quick in their judgments, he must make his answer to the Athenians, who are quick to repent of their judgments. He says that your poet is to have credit for many good services, having stopped you from being taken in too much by what foreigners say, or having pleasure from their flatteries, or belonging to Suckertown. Previously ambassadors from other cities used to take you in; they began calling you 'violet-garlanded', and as soon as that word was uttered, those garlands had you sitting on the tips of your backsides. And if to flatter you anyone called Athens 'glittering', that 'glittering' would get him anything he wanted, an epithet fit for praising sardines.

The speech goes on to say that the poet's reputation had reached the King of Persia, who had told the Spartans that the side which that man vituperated would win the war. That is why they are asking the Athenians to surrender Aegina; his home is there and they want to capture him. The anapaests end with six short lines, uttered without pause for breath, which defy and insult Cleon.

Resuming their character, the chorus sings, accompanied by the piper, an invocation to the Muse of Acharnae, followed by sixteen trochaic lines of declamation: adopting the guise of veterans of the Persian Wars they complain that clever young men entrap and entangle them in the law-courts. After a second song, which protests that those who fought at Marathon are now prosecuted by rascals, another sixteen lines continue the complaint about what happens in the courts.

Dikaiopolis briefly reappears to establish a market where Peloponnesians, Megarians and Boeotians can trade with him. The first to come is a starving Megarian, who hopes to sell his two daughters, disguised as piglets. An amusing scene follows, spiced by the fact that the word for 'piglet' was also a slang term for the female pudenda and by other ambiguities. An informer comes on, threatening to denounce the pigs as contraband, but is driven away. The chorus congratulate Dikaiopolis on the absence from his market of various Athenians, whom they accuse of unpleasant crimes and vices. A Boeotian, wishing to sell eels and other delicacies, is welcomed and his goods paid for by presenting him with another informer, who is trussed and packed up to be carried away as if he were a pottery vase, a familiar Athenian export. A messenger arrives from Lamachus, asking to buy some of the Boeotian fare with which to celebrate the festival of Anthesteria—a couple of months must have passed without our noticing—and is refused. Dikaiopolis carries the good things in, leaving the chorus to sing another pair of balanced songs, one rejecting war, the other welcoming Conciliation, who comes out in the guise of a beautiful woman.

As Dikaiopolis, out once more, makes preparations for a feast, a farmer, who has been ruined by the war, unavailingly asks for a drop of peace; then an emissary from a bridegroom brings a dish of meat from the wedding-feast, hoping for a cupful of peace in return, so that he may not have to leave his bride; he too is refused, but a bridesmaid, who comes with a whispered message, is more successful. Next a messenger arrives calling Lamachos to serve on the frontier, while another brings Dikaiopolis an invitation to dine with the priest of Dionysus. Line by line Lamachos calls for items of military equipment and Dikaiopolis for items of tasty food. Then they leave, one for the front, the other for dinner. After another pair of choral songs directed against a *choregos* who had failed to reward his singers with a dinner-party, a messenger announces (in a nonsensical parody of tragic style) that

Lamachus is a casualty. The general himself follows immediately, lamenting his wound in tragic language, while
Dikaiopolis comes back from his dinner with a girl on either
arm, and happily makes antiphonal responses, until he finally
leads the chorus out, raising a chant of victory for their play.

Victory is not yet assured; there are competing plays to
follow. At the end of the day the judges will give their decision.
They have been appointed by an elaborate method. Before
the contest the Council selected a number of names from each
of the ten 'tribes' between which the citizenry was divided,
and placed them in jars, one for each tribe. These were sealed
in the presence of the *choregoi*, to be reopened in the theatre
just before the performance. The presiding officer drew one
name from each jar and the ten chosen men swore to judge
impartially. When all the plays have been performed, each
man will write down his verdict, putting them in order of
merit, and cast it into another jar, from which the 'king' will
draw five at random. These will decide the issue, and in fact
Aristophanes, a young man in his early twenties, will be
crowned with the victor's wreath of ivy, beating into second
place Cratinus, the greatest of the dramatists of the earlier
generation. Eupolis, another rising young man, is third.

By making it uncertain whose voice would be effective, the
procedure was designed to minimise the possibility of bringing
threats or inducements to bear. Yet in the early fourth century,
at least, it was recognised that committed partisans might be
placed on the original panel. And since the judges' several
votes were made known, they were sometimes led to abandon
their own preferences by the way in which the plays were
popularly received. A philosopher like Plato might condemn
this, but they were judging not five plays *sub specie aeternitatis*
but particular performances of five plays: one of the aims of
the dramatist is to please his audience, and if he fails to do so,
there is something wrong with the play for that occasion.

The account of the play we have been watching has necessarily
been incomplete. Pure guesswork is the only way of supplying
many details. For instance, how much of the action took place

on the platform and how much did actors move on the space before it? Did all the extras, who played non-speaking parts, wear the comic actor's costume? Did they wear masks? When the chorus dropped their cloaks to come forward to address the audience, what was done with them? This part of the play was called the *parabasis*, or 'stepping-forward'. The name is applied both to the first element, usually anapaests, and more widely to the whole system including the songs and the trochaic addresses. The purpose of the stripping is generally supposed to be that of freeing their wearers for dancing. But if one wishes to imagine how and when they danced, there is neither agreement nor significant evidence. Movement of the arms and body was important, movement of the feet perhaps unnecessary. Even so, it is difficult to dance and speak at once. Hence some modern authors confidently state that the songs were sung by half-choruses, while the other half-chorus danced, that the anapaests were delivered by the chorus leader solo, and the trochaics by the leaders of half-choruses. It may have been standard practice so to divide the chorus, but evidence for it is frail.

There are, however, some uncertainties about which more can be said, and these are discussed in an appendix.

2

Aristophanes

THE play at which we have imagined ourselves to be spectators is in a sense typical of the nine plays that survive from about thirty which Aristophanes wrote before the end of the fifth century. Its principal elements recur again and again. Sometimes they are modified and they are not all to be found in all plays. There is no lack of novelty and experiment. But although *The Acharnians* was written when the poet was in his early twenties, it already clearly reveals his style and methods.

What may seem most important to the modern reader is the subject about which least need be said. This is not a place to insist on all the literary merits: the fantasy, the variety of incident, the abundance of jokes, their timing, their unexpectedness. Much, though not all, will come over in an English translation. Nevertheless there are other things which must be lost: the plays upon words; the parody of contemporary tragedy, often now only to be suspected, because the original is not preserved; and above all the charm of some of the lyric passages.

The primary object of this chapter is to look at Aristophanes' plays, not as timeless parts of world literature, but as constituents of life in Athens during the Peloponnesian War. The Athenians thought comedy important. It was publicly organised, supported by private generosity, given the incitement of competition for prizes between both authors and leading actors, and made part of two old religious festivals. *The Acharnians*, as we have seen, was produced at the midwinter Lenaia; the other festival, the City Dionysia, was held about the end of March. Since the sailing season began in the spring, there were in Athens at the time of the Dionysia men from the 'allied' states all over the Aegean; many would find a place in the theatre, including those who had brought the annual tribute. In his *Babylonians*, shown at the Dionysia in the year before *The Acharnians*, Aristophanes had criticised Athenian magistrates in the presence of these 'allies' and this caused Cleon, who was ridiculed in the play, to summon him before the Council on a charge of bringing the city into disrepute. No penalty seems to have been imposed, but one may notice that *Clouds* and *Birds*, other plays produced at the Dionysia, and *Women at the Thesmophoria*,[1] which may have been produced there, keep more or less clear of politically sensitive subjects, and *Peace* (421) is not critical of Athens (see below p. 34).

Clouds (423) is an attack on Socrates, but the play could be fully enjoyed by those who did not know him, for this dramatic Socrates is an individual who engages in all the antics that popular prejudice associated with intellectuals and keeps a school in which one can learn how to make a case, even in the law-courts, for cheating and violence. *Birds* (414), the most delightful of the plays, shows two men, Peisthetairos[2] and Euelpides, who wish to escape from life in the great city Athens. They come to the land of the birds, who form the chorus, dressed not uniformly but to represent twenty-four different species. The birds attack them but desist when persuaded that they can build a city in the sky which will sever communications between men and the gods, whose place they will take. This is done; Cloudcuckooland is founded and in the second half of the play Peisthetairos is pestered by a series of visitors from earth, not specifically from Athens, offering unwanted services or making requests. Emissaries come from the gods: Iris, who is contumeliously driven away; Prometheus, not an emissary, but a traitor, under cover of a sunshade, conveying a warning that the birds must insist on the surrender to them of the Queen, a lovely girl who guards Zeus' thunderbolts; finally a plenipotentiary embassy, consisting of the aristocratic Posidon, Heracles ready to accept any terms to get a dinner, and the barbarian Triballian god, who speaks gibberish. Posidon is outvoted, and Peisthetairos returns to the strains of a wedding-song with the Queen as his bride.

[1] The Thesmophoria was a religious festival.

[2] I do not share the confidence with which some scholars uphold their various normalisations of this name: Peithetairos, Peisetairos, Pisthetairos or Pithetairos.

THE COMIC THEATRE OF GREECE AND ROME

Euripides, the main subject of the *Women at the Thesmophoria* (411), was well known outside Athens. He disguises a kinsman as a woman to make his way into the feminine festival, where he has heard that the celebrants are to conspire against him in retaliation for his having exposed their vices through the evil women he had put upon the stage. The kinsman goes and speaks up ridiculously for Euripides, claiming that the dramatist had suppressed some of the most damaging facts. He is of course discovered, stripped, and fastened to a plank. The second half of the play contains a number of attempts by Euripides to rescue him, all involving parody of scenes from Euripidean tragedy. Finally the Scythian policeman who guards him and who speaks amusing broken Greek is lured away by a dancing-girl[1] introduced by Euripides in the disguise of an old bawd.

The plays from the Lenaia, on the other hand, generally have a close association with Athenian political life. In *Knights* (424) an elderly man Demos, who is the Athenian people, has fallen under the domination of his Paphlagonian slave, obviously Cleon, who manages him by bribery and bluster. Paphlagonia was a district of Asia Minor, and the name suggests the verb *paphlazein*, 'to bubble and splutter'. Another slave, whom it is tempting to identify with the general Demosthenes, calls in the help of the well-to-do young men who formed the Athenian cavalry, and they enter, riding pick-a-back on others who represent their horses. To depose the Paphlagonian it is necessary to find someone who will outdo him in vulgarity and lack of honesty. A suitable person is found in a sausage-seller, who wins a long contest with the Paphlagonian in reciprocal abuse and rival promises. Installed

[1] Although female speaking actors were unknown, it is possible that this silent character was played by a naked slave-girl. There are in Aristophanes several such silent characters whose part involves the excitation or (offstage) satisfaction of sexual desire. Sometimes the text implies that their private parts are visible and attractive. If they were played by men in tights, this might have raised a laugh. But a producer might have thought the titillation of real nudity more welcome. Some fourth-century vases made for the Greeks of Italy show naked female dancers or gymnasts in association with male actors who wear tights and masks.

in power, he rejuvenates Demos by boiling him in a cauldron, a traditional method of magicians. Thus the man who was the demagogue to beat all demagogues unexpectedly and inconsistently becomes a reformer who revives the glorious people of the young uncorrupted democracy, which was just, sensible and peace-loving.

Wasps (422) is a satire on the Athenian system of law. Philokleon, 'Cleon-lover', is shut up by his son Bdelykleon, 'Cleon-loather', to prevent him from going to sit as a juryman in the courts. Athenian juries were huge, normally having 501 members for public prosecutions, sometimes twice that number, drawn from a body of some 6,000 citizens registered as available for service, men to whom pay for sitting in court was often a valued source of income. They determined not only the verdict but also the sentence. Philokleon loves the power this gives him over the accused. His attempts to escape from his house occupy the opening of the play. Then his fellow-jurymen, who form the chorus, come to bring him away to the courts. Finding him imprisoned, they cast off their cloaks for action, revealing themselves as having the form of wasps with menacing stings. They are repulsed and Bdelykleon compensates his father by allowing him to try a domestic case at home, that of a dog accused of stealing food. As evening comes on and the courts are closed, Philokleon is encouraged to go out to a party, from which he returns drunk, bringing a girl he has stolen and pursued by a man and a woman he has assaulted, who threaten him with the law.

The repeated attacks upon Cleon invite a number of questions. Were they due to rancour over his reaction to the *Babylonians*, or to disagreement with his policies? Were they likely to be welcomed by the majority of the audience? Did Aristophanes intend to influence public opinion or simply to amuse his hearers by a caricature?

In theory it is unjustifiable to assume that any opinions expressed in a play are those of the dramatist himself; much erroneous interpretation of ancient drama has been advanced by critics who have ascribed to the author views which he put into the mouth of a character. Nevertheless Aristophanic comedy has features by which some opinions can be identified as being his own, or at the least as being those he wished his audience to believe he held. One is the fact that in the ana-paests which introduce the *parabasis* the chorus usually does not speak in its own character, but openly claims to be the poet's mouthpiece (see p. 22). Another is the repeated introduction of certain sentiments and the repeated ridicule of certain politicians, while contrary views are discredited, if mentioned at all, and politicians of another kind escape attack; the poet does not seem to be politically unprejudiced. We may be sure that Aristophanes appeared and wished to appear to hold certain views; we cannot prove that this was not a cynical pretence, but nothing suggests such dishonesty.

There was a tradition that a poet was a teacher, and more than once Aristophanes makes the claim for himself in serious contexts. The first occasion is in *The Acharnians*, where the chorus declares that 'he will teach you many good lessons to bring you happiness, not flattering, nor holding out hopes of pay, nor deceiving you', that is, not acting like the crooked politicians (656). The last is in *Frogs*, written when defeat in the war was imminent; the chorus of deceased initiates into the holy mysteries of Eleusis, who enjoy a favoured lot in the next world, say that it is right that the sacred chorus should give the city good advice: all citizens should have the same civic rights, there should be an amnesty for past offences, and citizenship given to all who will man the ships. The advice ascribed to these honourable and disinterested figures must be advice with which the poet associates himself. It is said to have been so popular that the play was, quite exceptionally, given a second performance.

Here we see Aristophanes making liberal and generous proposals certainly intended to influence opinion. But this was consistent with attachment to some social concepts that were current among upper-class conservatives. He follows them in dividing the citizens into *chrēstoi*, or 'good men', and *ponēroi*, or 'bad men'. The former were on the whole men of means, of 'good' family, of good education in the traditional athletic and literary disciplines, and it was they who ought to be elected as 'generals'[1] and be the policy-makers whose

[1] The ten generals, elected annually and eligible for re-election, not only provided military and naval commanders but also had a

advice the people should follow. The latter were the upstarts; some had made money by trade or the employment of slaves as artisans; they entered politics for their own enrichment and secured power by posing as champions of the people, whose favour they secured by making them payments from state funds.

Aristophanes' political sympathies were with these conservatives. The chorus of *Frogs*, quoted above, continues:

> Among the citizens there are some we know to be well-born, well-behaved honest gentlemen, educated in the wrestling-schools and in dancing and the arts of the Muses; these we ill-treat but use for all purposes foreigners and red-heads and rascally sons of rascally fathers, new arrivals, men whom the city would once not have been willing to use even as scapegoats. But even now, O ye foolish men, use the good sort once again.

Twenty years earlier, in *Knights*, he had declared the same sympathies. The rich young cavalrymen assert that 'our poet hates the men we hate and he dares to speak the right'. Cleon was the butt of that play because he was one of the new men of the people who had broken the dominance of the old families.

In the year when *Knights*, later claimed by Aristophanes as 'a blow in the belly', won first prize Cleon was re-elected general. The play did not succeed in undermining his popular support. It may cause surprise that Aristophanes, writing for a mass audience, so consistently turned his ridicule against the new men who had the favour of so large a part of the citizenry. It may be guessed that, although the audience for comedy was very large, it was not proportionately representative, but that the half of the people who were absent from the theatre were on the whole the poorer half, who preferred to spend the payment from the theoric fund on food and drink; the followers of men like Cleon and Hyperbolus may there have been in

---

general influence on policy because of a wide responsibility for finance and the right to summon the assembly and put proposals to it.

a minority. Some support for this guess may be found in the fact that Aristophanes' rival Eupolis shared his social outlook, if his own view is to be seen in a fragment which asserts that 'our generals once were chosen from the greatest families, men pre-eminent by wealth and birth ... so our affairs went without mishap. Now we elect scum as generals and our campaigns go as they do.'

There is another consideration. The followers of the demagogues did not necessarily admire them without reservation. They may have believed them to be in politics for what they could make, but have supported them because of their promises. This would not preclude envy and they may have enjoyed any personal discomfort suffered in the theatre by those for whom it would profit them to vote.

The other two plays belonging to the Lenaia, *Lysistrata* (411) probably and *Frogs* (405) certainly, were written in times of crisis, when partisan politics would have been out of place. *Lysistrata* is discussed below (p. 36); in *Frogs* the poet turns his back on the world of impending defeat and possible destruction to a most entertaining critique of the tragedians Aeschylus and Euripides, who was but recently dead. Missing him, Dionysus goes to the underworld to bring him back. The first part of the play has the god's adventures on a sometimes perilous journey, which include having to pull an oar in Charon's boat on the Styx and to compete as he does so with a chorus of frogs.[1] After further difficulties, arising from the fact that he has disguised himself as Heracles, he finally enters the palace of Pluto, and the chorus, now dressed as Eleusinian initiates, deliver the *parabasis*. Next news comes that Euripides has laid claim to the tragic throne of Aeschylus and that Dionysus, with his long experience of the theatre, has been appointed judge. There follows a lengthy contest between the two poets over the merits of their art, a contest punctuated by inept comments from Dionysus. He cannot decide between them, but Pluto urges him to pick one of the two and take him back to earth. Thus we return to the original purpose of his descent

[1] There is to my mind a strong case for believing the frogs to have appeared in the orchestra; see K. J. Dover, *Aristophanic Comedy* (London, 1972), pp. 177-8.

to the underworld. He determines to take the one who offers the city the better advice. Euripides is not at a loss for a rhetorical antithesis and a far-fetched stratagem; Aeschylus is more reluctant but more realistic and unexpectedly gets Dionysus' verdict.

It is a striking fact that the mass audience was able to appreciate a play with this literary subject. More than that its abnormal structure makes them no concessions. Disconnected scenes of knockabout humour usually succeeded the *parabasis*, while the more serious part of the play came before it. In *Frogs* the pattern is reversed: Dionysus' misadventures have a large physical element, while the latter part of the play is on an intellectual level and concerned with a single subject.

But there is some danger of exaggerating the crowd's literary understanding. Although some serious points are made, they are not made by themselves in isolation. The parody of Euripides' monodies scores some undoubted hits on his style and metrical liberties. But to enjoy the parody a knowledge of Euripides' more recent plays or the niceties of metre would not have been necessary; it would have been enough to understand that the language of the tragic stage was being used to lament a trivial domestic loss. Even so Aeschylus was made to bring on the 'Muse of Euripides', either a highly made-up man or a naked slave-girl, who postured for the audience's diversion while he sang his travesty.

Consider by contrast the attack on Euripides' prologues. Aeschylus alleges that the phrase 'lost his little oil-flask' can be interpolated into their first sentences. He demonstrates this by using the phrase to complete the third line of three plays, the second of two, and the first of another. This is very amusing, as the fatal words are introduced earlier and earlier, but it has no value as literary criticism. No aesthetic sensibility is required to see the joke.

The praises of peace are sung by Aristophanes in several of his plays, but to praise peace and to be a pacifist are different things. 'War is for the sake of peace,' wrote Aristotle (*Pol.* 1333 a 35). Most people always want peace, but not peace at any price. They want peace with victory or at least with safety. The route to peace may lie through war. Men can regret that, but they recognise it.

To see *The Acharnians* as a manifesto in favour of peace is too simple. Most Athenians wanted peace, but they wanted it on their own terms. There was at this time no hope of a compromise, as had been made plain when in 430 they had tried to open negotiations. The coalition opposing them wished and hoped to destroy the Athenian Empire; the Athenians were determined to maintain it. For anything we know, Aristophanes shared this ambition. In his next play, *Knights*, the rejuvenated people is hailed as 'monarch of Greece'. He had no suggestion of how to make peace a practical policy. All he does is to play with a fantasy of peace. His Dikaiopolis has no care for national interests, or indeed for any interests but his own. How delightful it is to imagine oneself for a moment as enjoying the pleasures of selfishness! But this is no more than a holiday escape from reality. It is impossible for an individual to contract out of his country's war and, even if it were possible, peace cannot be made, as Dikaiopolis made it, without any terms except that it is to last for thirty years.

Yet in a way *The Acharnians* had a political purpose. The Athenians were not agreed about the terms on which they would be ready to make peace. Aristophanes seems to have been one of those who believed that the Peloponnesian War ought to have been avoided and ought to be brought to an end. He suggested therefore that its origins had been trivial, that the blame did not rest entirely with Sparta, and that if the two great powers co-operated, they could rule the Greek world. If his play could exert any influence, it would be in favour of moderates who were ready to accept some compromise if the opportunity offered. At the same time he tried to discredit those who favoured fighting on for decisive victory by accusing them of making personal gains from the war.

Peace, of 421, may have been begun to urge an end to hostilities, but concluded to celebrate it. The war had lasted for ten years; the coalition had failed to reduce Athens and its Spartan leaders were anxious to recover the 120 front-line soldiers taken prisoner in 425 and used by the Athenians as hostages to keep their farms free from further invasion. On the other hand the Athenian attempt to instigate a revolution in Boeotia, their northern neighbour, had led to their army's rout at Delium. The contest might seem to be drawn and peace on terms of the *status quo* possible. By the time that Aristophanes' play was acted, it was known that formal ratification of a treaty was on the point of taking place. But it proved to be a fragile peace, since the issue had not been settled. Although some, both in Athens and in Sparta, hoped that the two states would co-operate to impose order on the other Greeks, the Athenians took every opportunity to weaken the Spartan position, while for various reasons the Boeotians, Megarians and Corinthians refused to adhere to the treaty.

The hero of the play, Trygaios, flies up to heaven on the back of a giant dung-beetle—a crane will have lifted him up from behind the *skene* to deposit him in front of it—and there finds that Zeus has gone and that the god War is preparing to pound the Greeks to pieces. Advised by Hermes, he calls for a panhellenic effort to draw the goddess Peace out of the cave in which she has been incarcerated. No doubt Aristophanes realised that the right way to peace lay through unity and was sincere in raising his voice in its favour. But he knew quite well that the way would not be followed. When the chorus enter and begin to haul upon ropes to draw Peace out, it soon appears that the Boeotians, the Argives, the military party among the Spartans, the Megarians and many Athenians are not joining in the effort. The work is left to the farmers, who finally succeed in extricating her.

The rest of the play consists predominantly of a protracted celebration of peace with praise of the joys of country life, now once again possible. Sacrifice is made to the goddess and the climax is a wedding-party, the marriage of Trygaios and Opōra, 'Harvest', one of her attendants, the other, Theōria or 'Spectacle', having been given to the Council.

Clearly this is no more than an agreeable fantasy. Co-operation between the Greek cities was necessary to secure peace; it was not to be won by the efforts of farmers, let alone by those of the Athenian farmers, with whom the chorus becomes identified. Perhaps simple-minded members of the audience might regard the second half of the play as a celebration of the peace that was about to be concluded, and the

35

author may have been ready to make use of the short-sighted enthusiasm for it, but the first half shows that he had no illusions about its prospects.

It is interesting that the blessings of peace are those of country life. At least three-quarters of Athenian citizens owned some land (Dion. Hal. *Lysias* 32). For many it may have been no more than a patch which could not provide a living, but which gave them a basis that could be supplemented, preferably by pay for activities proper for citizens, attendance at the assembly, service on juries or in the navy. So the majority of the spectators will have had connections with the country and been ready to place themselves on the side of the larger farmers.

Perhaps *Lysistrata*, produced early in 411, was designed to exert a real influence for peace. In the summer of 413 the disastrous end of the expedition to Syracuse had inflicted immense losses both of men and of ships. During the following winter neutral states hastened to join what they thought was the winning side, the Athenian 'allies' revolted, and there was a general expectation that the summer of 412 would see final victory (Thucydides 8.1). But it did not; the Athenians made heroic efforts and, although they had lost their undisputed command of the sea, succeeded in keeping control of Samos and of the essential passage of corn-ships from the Black Sea. Yet although their enemies had failed to press home their advantage, the outlook was threatening. If immediate peace had been possible, it would surely have been welcomed. But was peace on tolerable terms available? The rather inadequate evidence of Thucydides' unfinished eighth book suggests that whereas some thought that negotiations should be opened at once, others considered that this would be taken as a sign of weakness (this was indeed to be the reaction of the Spartan king Agis) and that the war should for the time be continued. In these circumstances to call attention to the hardships suffered by women, separated from their husbands who were on active service, may have been intended to aid the peace-party.

Yet Aristophanes cannot have supposed that an acceptable peace was to be had for the asking, any more than he can have supposed that his suggested method of bringing the Greeks to their senses was anything other than a fantasy. And a hilarious fantasy it is. The citizen women of the warring states enter, with some reluctance, into a compact to refuse their husbands sexual relations until they make peace. This is inconsequential, for shortly before they were complaining that they were deprived of sex by their husbands' absence. But such inconsequentiality is typical of Aristophanic comedy. Unhampered by need to be consistent, the dramatist can freely develop each idea with which his imagination presents him.

The Athenian women go further, seizing the Acropolis, which they hold against the police and the old men, who try to re-establish masculine authority. The deprived men, who for the purposes of the play seem never to have heard of slave prostitutes or even of masturbation, to which the more practical women intended to resort, are immediately afflicted by continuous erection, which the phallus of the comic actor's costume could represent in exaggerated form. An embassy, racked by this torment, comes from Sparta and the two sides, reminded of how they had in earlier times aided one another, quickly agree; they hardly trouble to argue about territorial claims, being more concerned with the attractions of a beautiful girl whose name is Reconciliation. The play ends with a joyful song and dance. This is nothing but a fanciful wish in a dream world. The Athenians would have been happy if their ambitions for empire could have been wiped from the Greek memory, to be replaced by a sentimental regard for old and better days. But when the festival was over, they had to face reality.

We do not know how *Lysistrata* was received. To argue from silence is dangerous, but it may be that the reason why there is no record is that it was not placed among the first three comedies at the Lenaia of 411.

Like other authors of Old Comedy, Aristophanes made it his practice to ridicule and malign living contemporaries. Was this intended to hurt and to damage, to excite the laughter of contempt? It is quite possible to make friendly fun of others, who may enjoy the joke. Politicians collect caricatures of themselves drawn in this spirit. But I doubt whether many of Aristophanes' butts relished the prominence he gave them, or that he was not moved by malice. 'Taking pleasure in what goes wrong for others' is a feeling for which the Greeks had a word (*epichairekakia*), and one which his audience will have known and enjoyed. His victims are accused of frigid writing, cowardice, effeminacy, passive homosexuality, adultery, stench, blackmail, peculation and other acts and qualities which are not subjects of kindly fun. This makes one suppose that allusions to ugliness, obesity and poverty were intended to raise a laugh at the man's expense and one in which he would not readily join. The runner in the torch-race who had let himself go flabby and came trailing in distressed, urged on by a rain of slaps from the spectators, would not welcome being reminded of that spectacle as much as the Athenians who had been amused by his humiliation (*Frogs* 1089 ff.).

There are three persons often attacked by Aristophanes who are still living figures for us: Cleon, Euripides and Socrates. No doubt can exist that he hated Cleon, both for personal reasons, since the politician had attempted to retaliate when first assailed, and because he saw in him an upstart demagogue who won power by bribing the people from public funds, and was moreover a man who preferred war to peace. Cleon's reprisals suggest that he thought the attacks dangerous. But he need not have worried, since the Athenian populace was not fickle in its favour to him.

Whereas it is not possible to detect any sympathy for Cleon in the works of Aristophanes, the case is not so clear with regard to Euripides. The most serious complaints he levels against him are that his dramas are full of sexually immoral women and that his characters, male and female, free and slave, talk and talk and argue and get new ideas. This is not only untragic; it also sets a bad example. Euripides would not feel this to be adverse criticism; he intended his plays to be like that and a great many people liked them like that.

For the rest, the frequent use of Euripidean lines in new and unsuitable contexts or their quotation in some distorted form could be taken as a compliment. It showed with what attention Aristophanes heard or read his plays and how it could be assumed that many of the audience were familiar with them too. The repeated joke about ragged heroes, used by other writers of comedy also, becomes funny by virtue of repetition, and Euripides may almost have acquired credit by having provided its occasion. Intellectually Aristophanes probably disapproved of his way of writing tragedy, but he would have been ready to echo Dionysus: 'I think Aeschylus wise, but my delight is in Euripides.'

Since Socrates is an established hero to the modern world, Aristophanes' treatment of him is sometimes not taken at its face value. Plato's fictional account in the *Symposium*, which makes them both present at a party in honour of the tragic poet Agathon, another man of whom Aristophanes made fun, is said to show that all three were good friends. But in the *Apology* Plato declares his belief that the *Clouds* had been a cause of prejudice against Socrates, contributory to his condemnation. And it is hard to avoid the conclusion that the play was intended to damage him. It was harmless ridicule to represent him as running a school whose pupils were shut up away from the fresh air, explaining which end of a gnat was responsible for its whine, investigating the path of the moon, and riding in a suspended basket because:

> If from the ground below I had researched on
> What lies above, I'd never have found it. No,
> The earth attracts by force to its own self
> The moisture of one's thought. The same thing happens
> With cress.

All this is a caricature of the intellectual, imagined by the ordinary man to be an unhealthy and eccentric crackpot pursuing useless enquiries. The picture was simply untrue of Socrates, but it did not represent him as dangerous. More serious was the accusation that he worshipped, not Zeus, but Clouds and Air and Cosmic Whirl. Even worse was to make him the owner of an Immoral Argument which defeated Moral Argument. It does not matter that the contest between the two is conducted and concluded in comic terms: Immoral Argument wins when Moral Argument is forced to admit that every man in the audience has been a catamite, and impulsively deserts to join the overwhelming majority. Audiences enjoy being made the subject of preposterously exaggerated insults, and the Athenians would not suppose that Aristophanes approved the result of the contest. Its consequences are seen when the young Pheidippides is made a pupil of the victor, unwillingly consenting but traditionally obedient, and returns to beat his father and to prove it right to do so. This is what comes of Socratic education. The play ends with the setting fire, at the instigation of the god Hermes, to Socrates' house, in an attempt on his life and that of his pupils. This scene, not harmless ridicule but incitement to violence, was first introduced into the unfinished revised version of the play, which had had only limited success at its original performance, coming third. It looks as if Aristophanes hoped, by sharpening his attack upon Socrates, to win greater favour. He may or may not have shared popular misconceptions about him, but as a dramatist he saw that they could be used to make an entertaining play.

3

Old Comedy

THE term 'Old Comedy' means comedy produced in Athens during the fifth century BC. Antiquity regarded Eupolis, Cratinus and Aristophanes as its leading exponents, but had no doubt that Aristophanes was the greatest of the three. We are not in a position to test that judgment, which led to the survival of eleven of his plays and none of theirs. But Eupolis was still being copied and read in Egypt in the fourth century AD and Cratinus in the second or third. This must surely have been due to literary merit as well as the interest they had for admirers of classical Greece.

In *Knights* (424 BC) Aristophanes paid tribute to the power of Cratinus in his prime, when like a river in flood, he had 'swept away oaks and planes and had uprooted his enemies', while his lyrics were sung at every dinner-party. But he had gone to pieces with advancing years and drink. He deserved to be pensioned off, Aristophanes suggested, with free wine in the prytaneum and a seat in the theatre alongside Dionysus himself. The next year however Cratinus made his come-back, when his *Pytinē* or *Flask* beat Aristophanes' *Clouds*. In it he introduced himself as married to Comedy, who complained that he was deserting her for Drink; 'once I was his wife, but am no longer'. His friends came and urged her not to bring an action against him for ill-treatment. A few surviving lines suggest a project of reforming the erring poet:

> Now how could one put an end to his drinking, to his drinking too much? I know. I will break his bottles and smash his flagons to pieces, as if they were hit by a thunderbolt, and every single other vessel too that he uses for drinking; he shan't keep even a saucer with a taste of wine.

But a reconciliation seems to have followed, when someone urged that a poet's inspiration was in wine, not water.

41

O Lord Apollo, how his verses flow! There is splashing from his fountains, his mouth is the Twelve Springs themselves, Ilissus is in his throat. What more can one say? Unless someone puts a gag in his mouth, he will swamp the whole place with his lines.

Eupolis' dramatic career fell entirely within the course of the Peloponnesian War. Fourteen plays by him were known to later scholars and of these no fewer than seven had won the first prize. He seems to have shared the dislike shown by Aristophanes, of whom he was an almost exact contemporary, for the new lower-class leaders of the democracy. He claimed indeed to have helped in the composition of *Knights*, perhaps an accusation of plagiarism, while Aristophanes charged him, in the revised version of *Clouds* (553–6), with having villainously distorted *Knights* to attack the 'demagogue' Hyperbolus in his play *Marikās*, 'to which he had added a drunken old woman to dance the kordax,[1] a character produced long ago by Phrynichus'. Phrynichus was another contemporary, whose first play was performed in 429.

One cannot help asking whether the surviving plays of Aristophanes can be taken as typical of those of 'Old Comedy'. Scanty as are the remains of its other authors, there is enough to show that in many ways he either followed previous practice, or did what other poets of his time were doing.

In the first place it is clear that the Aristophanic choruses were in an established tradition. Most frequently the chorus gave the comedy its name. We know of plays entitled *Goats*, *Griffins*, *Ants*, *Bees*, etc. which correspond to his *Wasps*, *Birds* and *Frogs*. In others the chorusmen were, as in some of his, made to represent women, *Runaway Women*, *Women from Thrace*, *Old Women*. Then there were personifications, to be compared with the *Clouds*: *Wealths*, *Demes*, *Costumes*.

Nor was the *parabasis*, that interruption of the action when the chorus addresses itself to the spectators, his invention; it appeared in some plays by Cratinus, who belonged to the previous generation, as well as by his contemporary Eupolis and others with whom he competed. There is enough evidence to show that Aristophanes was not the originator of the

[1] A vulgar dance.

symmetrical scheme that is most fully displayed in his four earliest plays and in *The Birds*. It has five elements: (1) anapaests; (2) a song (*ōdē*); (3) sixteen or twenty long trochaic lines (*epirrhēma*); (4) another song (*antōdē*) metrically corresponding to the first; (5) sixteen or twenty long trochaic lines (*antepirrhēma*).

The other poets used the introductory anapaests, as he usually did, to speak in their own person, praising themselves and attacking their rivals. There are several passages which apologise for this and suggest that this use was an innovation. It is certainly not likely to have been a primitive feature, but was more probably the consequence of competition between dramatists in the theatre. Nor were anapaests *de rigeur* metrically; Eupolis sometimes substituted, as did Aristophanes in *Clouds*, a metre which goes by his name, and there are traces of other variants.

It may be guessed that another formal pattern found in many of Aristophanes' plays, although not in *The Acharnians*, did not originate with him. This pattern belongs to what modern scholars call the *Agōn* or Contest. Representatives of opposed points of view are pitted against one another and put their case in turn, interrupted by heckling mainly from their adversary, but also from a character who acts the buffoon. Their speeches, which often end with a *pnīgos* or passage delivered without pause for breath, are each introduced by a song and encouragement from the chorus, which sometimes concludes the *Agōn* by giving a verdict. In its most perfected form this *Agōn* is almost exactly symmetrical. Thus in *Birds* the two songs correspond syllable for syllable, the speeches of encouragement each consist of two anapaestic tetrameters, and each of the subsequent speeches, heckling counted, occupies sixty-one anapaestic tetrameters followed by sixteen anapaestic dimeters. To be accurate, that play shows what may be called the form of the *Agōn* without providing a true contest, since Peisthetairos champions the same cause in both halves. But in *Knights*, where the Paphlagonian and the sausage-seller are genuine opponents, correspondence is only marginally less strict.

Most plays by Aristophanes contain allusions to politics; several are based on the contemporary situation and would be unthinkable without it. That he was not alone in this involvement with the affairs of the city is illustrated by the *Demes* of Eupolis. Written for production in 412, soon after the disaster at Syracuse had faced Athens with the prospect of destruction, it showed the great statesmen of the past called up from the underworld to advise the city in her hour of need. There are some enigmatic but significant fragments from the *parabasis*. First from the *antōdē*:

> Then they say that Peisandros was twisted[1] yesterday when at breakfast, because he refused to provide meals for a foreigner who had no food.
> And Pauson went up to Theogenes as he was making his dinner to his heart's content off one of his own ships, gave him a hiding once for all, and a good twisting; and Theogenes lay paralysed and farting all night.
> Now Callias ought to be twisted and those in the Long Walls with him, for they breakfast better than we do.

Clearly this was a time of food-shortage; the first two men attacked were well-known gluttons, and the third was rich, whereas Pauson is twice mentioned by Aristophanes as a starveling and once called a 'thorough villain'.

The *antepirrhēma* accuses some demagogue, perhaps Hyperbolus, of not being of Attic birth, of having been a male prostitute, and of having proposed to treat as criminals certain generals who had wished to pay heed to divine warnings against sending an expedition to Mantinea, probably the unsuccessful one of 418.

The ridicule of individuals was a feature common to all the dramatists about whom there is any quantity of evidence. Many of Aristophanes' victims are to be found also in the fragments of his rivals. At least three other comic poets made a butt of Socrates. Eupolis frag. 352 runs:

> I hate Socrates too, that beggarly chatterer, who has thought of everything except where his next meal is coming from.

---

[1] The meaning of the Greek word is disputed. It may refer to a method of torture, but some plausibly think it means 'buggered'.

Politicians—Pericles, Cleon, Hyperbolus and others—are
lampooned. Later critics constantly refer to these personal
attacks as a prime characteristic of Old Comedy. Not only
that, but they tend to regard them as justified and salutary.
Horace writes (*Satires* 1.4.1–5):

> The poets Eupolis and Cratinus and Aristophanes and the
> other great men who created antique comedy felt no
> restraint against branding anyone who deserved to be
> noticed because he was a bad character and a thief, or an
> adulterer or assassin or of ill-repute in any other way.

This description seems particularly suited to Cratinus who,
according to a late anonymous author, 'added utility to the
charm of comedy, by denouncing evil-doers and punishing
them by a public flogging in his comedies'. Although Horace
gives an exaggerated impression of the poets' moral purpose
and the wickedness of those they attacked, he does not fall
into the error of treating their attitude as one of affectionate
raillery. They wished to exploit unpopularity and eccentricity.

It is a fact to be insisted upon that not only did Aristophanes
relate the alleged vices or ridicule the habits and actions of the
same persons in play after play, but the other dramatists also
pursued them. They had become stock figures of comic drama
and references to them were for that reason the more effective
with the audience. Men like novelty, but they also like what is
familiar. In the end they can tire of the latter, but its attraction
is far from ephemeral. It pleased the Athenian audience to be
reminded of their contempt for Cleonymus, who was said to
have dropped his shield and run, and they will not have
minded how often they heard of his disgrace.

Similarly there were stock motifs repeated from play to
play. Here it is easy to find modern parallels from the more
undemanding plays and cartoons—the interfering mother-in-
law and the henpecked husband forced to wash up at the
kitchen sink. Several times Aristophanes pretends that he did
not descend to such elementary material. For example:

> If it is reasonable to honour someone who has become the
> best and most famous producer of comedy of all mankind,
> our poet declares himself to be worthy of great praise.

First of all he is the only man who has put a stop to his rivals always making fun of rags and waging war on lice; and then those Heracleses kneading their bread and always hungry, he was the first to bring them into disrepute and drive them out of the theatre, and he got rid of those slaves they used to bring on howling, so that a fellow-slave could jeer at their stripes and then put a question like this: 'You poor wretch, what has happened to your skin? You don't say that a whip has invaded your ribs in force and used your back for some practice in tree-felling?'

These particular motifs did not occur in *Peace*, from which this passage is taken (734–47), but most of them can be found in other plays by him. Aristophanes did not dispense with the stock themes used by comic dramatists; he knew that his audience loved them. It may be that he relied less on their intrinsic funniness, and preferred to use them as an element in other jokes. The beginning of *Frogs* illustrates this. Dionysus enters with his slave Xanthias, who rides on a donkey, carrying a huge bundle on a pole over his shoulder.

> *Xanthias.* Master, shall I say one of the usual things, at which the spectators always laugh?
> *Dionysus.* Anything you like, except 'It's crushing me'. Keep off that. It makes me quite sick.
> *Xanthias.* No other witty remark?
> *Dionysus.* Anything but 'I'm being squeezed'.
> *Xanthias.* What then? Shall I make that really funny joke?
> *Dionysus.* By all means. Go ahead. There's just one thing you're not to say.
> *Xanthias.* What?

Dionysus bans a couple of indecent jokes, after which Xanthias continues: 'Why had I to carry all these traps, if I'm not going to do any of the things Phrynichus and Lycis and Ameipsias used to do?' No doubt when Xanthias shortly afterwards exclaimed: 'It's crushing my shoulder', that got a laugh.

There is in Aristophanes a great deal of sexual, and some scatological, obscenity. The fragments we have of his contemporaries' plays confirm his assertion that they too indulged in it. Some modern writers have tried to palliate this by finding a religious origin in ritual obscenity and maintaining that it was traditional and proper at the festival of Dionysus. If there is any truth in the theory, the spectators will have expected to be entertained in this way, because it had always been part of the programme. But what they expected was entertainment, not a religious ceremony.

The Greek sense of propriety will not have coincided with our own, but for many, if not for most, some sense of shame attached to sexual acts and to defecation. If it had not, there would have been no need to use euphemisms in literature to replace what correspond to our four-letter words. In so far as Greek Old Comedy talks openly about bodily parts and normal acts which were probably not usual subjects of general conversation, it may have provided a relief from inhibitions. The relief will have been all the greater if these acts could be made to appear absurd and laughable by exaggeration and by attaching jokes to them. There is much of this in Aristophanes.

But there is another side. Clearly a fifth-century audience, or a large part of it, was ready to laugh at things in which most readers of this book probably do not find a source of amusement such as incontinence of the bowels and sodomy. We may enjoy jokes about them, but do not regard them as funny in themselves. Similarly we can jest about madmen, but do not, like our eighteenth-century ancestors, visit madhouses for our entertainment.

Aristophanes was not alone in providing much entertainment by parody of tragedy and allusions to it. His methods are still used by comedians, but he had the advantage that his audience was an audience of tragedy-goers, who would see tragedies at the same festival and in the same theatre as his comedies. The simplest form of parody was the introduction of vocabulary drawn from tragedy, which used much language that was not ordinary Attic speech. Put in the mouth of a down-to-earth character, this was comically inappropriate, especially if he mixed it with everyday phrases and colloquialisms. Sometimes metres were used whose traditional place was in serious poetry and even the iambic trimeter, the most common metre for dialogue, could be made to adhere to the stricter rules employed in tragedy and so suggest an incongruous elevation of style.

Parody becomes more specific when actual lines are borrowed from a tragedian, either verbatim, when the fun lies in their transference to the comic contest, or with the substitution or addition of a word or phrase with ridiculous effect. The more apposite the line in its new setting, the sharper is the impact of the joke, and the greater the admiration for the cleverness of the comic poet. A most successful and sustained instance is in *Frogs*, when Euripides is discomfited by Dionysus' use of lines which he had himself written.

> *Dionysus.* My choice shall fall on him my soul
>   desires.   1468
> *Euripides.* Remembering the gods and solemn oath
>   You swore to bring me home, now choose
>   your friend.   1470
> *Dionysus.* My tongue is sworn—but I'll choose
>   Aeschylus.
> *Euripides.* What have you done, man? You foul
>   blackguard!
> *Dionysus.*   I?
>   I judged a win for Aeschylus. Why not?
> *Euripides.* How can you face me, wreaking a deed
>   of shame?
> *Dionysus.* What's shameful, if the audience think
>   not so?   1475
> *Euripides.* Will you do nothing, wretch, and see
>   me dead?
> *Dionysus.* Who knows if life be death and death
>   be life,
>   To breathe to dine, and sleep a sheepskin
>   rug?

Lines 1471 and 1475 distort verses from Euripides' plays that had become notorious:

> My tongue is sworn—my mind did never swear

and

> What's shameful, if the doers think not so?

1477 is known to be taken verbatim. 1469–70 look like another distortion and it would not be surprising if 1468 and 1474 proved also to be from him.

There is, however, one way in which Aristophanes' surviving plays do not give a fair picture of Old Comedy. They do not fully represent its range of theme; in particular they include no example of a play that treated a story from mythology in a comic manner. Such became increasingly popular and Aristophanes himself wrote several which have not survived. Fortunately much of the plot of Cratinus' *Dionysalexandros* is known. In it part of the story usually attached to the Trojan prince Paris, *alias* Alexander, was transferred to the god Dionysus. The summary given in a papyrus runs as follows:

> . . . Hermes leaves. They (probably satyrs) talk with the spectators (i.e. the audience) about the poets and make fun of Dionysus when he comes on the scene . . . Hera offers him an unshaken despotic rule, Athena good luck in war, Aphrodite promises that he should be very beautiful and attractive. He adjudges her the winner, and then sailing to Lacedaemon he returns with Helen to Ida (the Trojan mountain). Shortly afterwards he hears that the Achaeans (Greeks) are burning the country . . . Alexander. Quickly hiding Helen in a basket, he transforms himself into a ram and awaits events. Alexander comes on the scene, discovers them, and orders them both to be taken to the ships, intending to hand them over to the Achaeans. Helen is unwilling to go; pitying her, he keeps her to be his wife, but sends Dionysus off to be surrendered. The satyrs follow the god, telling him to be of good cheer and promising never to desert him.

The summary concludes with the words: 'Pericles is ridiculed by innuendo as having brought war on the Athenians.' This note, which suggests 430 as the date, is valuable evidence that mythological subjects did not exclude contemporary political references. Another example of this is provided by the same author's *Cheirones*, or *Cheiron and Co.*, fragments from which refer to Pericles and his mistress Aspasia, but without naming them. 'Discord and old Cronos lay together and engendered a mighty despot, whom the gods called head-raiser . . . and Lewdness bore Hera for him, a bitch-eyed mistress.' Zeus was called 'cloud-raiser' (*nephelēgeretās*) and Pericles, who had a very high skull, is here suggested by *kephalēgeretās*, 'head-raiser'; Hera was *boōpis*, 'cow-eyed', replaced here by *kynōpis*, 'bitch-eyed'.

There seem also to have been plays which included realistic scenes from contemporary life, to be contrasted with Aristophanic fantasy; they are marked by quiet humour rather than broad jests.

> *A.* I've come from the bath-house quite boiled, and my throat's parched.
> *B.* I'll give you something to drink.
> *A.* My God, my spittle's sticky.
> *B.* What shall I use to mix your drink in? The little cup?
> *A.* No, no! Not the little one. It makes me feel sick at once, ever since I drank medicine out of one like that. Fill up mine now, the bigger one.

> * * *

> *A.* Undrinkable, Glyke!
> *Glyke.* Did she put in too much water?
> *A.* Worse! It's nothing but water!
> *Glyke.* What have you done? Damn you, what measures did you use?
> *B.* Two of water, mamma.
> *Glyke.* And of wine?
> *B.* Four.
> *Glyke.* Devil take you! Frogs are what you should mix drinks for.[1]

This comes from Pherecrates' *Corianno*, probably written during the Peloponnesian War. Corianno, in all likelihood to be

[1] A normal mixture would have been two of water to *one* of wine. To drink wine neat or as good as neat was a mark of dissipation.

identified with 'A' in these lines, was a courtesan, but it is uncertain whether she was a real inhabitant of Athens or a fictitious person. Pherecrates is said not to have indulged in personal abuse, but to have been 'inventive of plots'. This suggests that he was a forerunner of the direction which was to be taken by comedy in the following century.

An immense amount has been written about the origins of Old Comedy. Some critics, with whom I incline to agree, consider that this has been largely misdirected effort, because there is so little hard evidence. The earliest plays to survive were written fifty years after the introduction of comedy at the City Dionysia and their form may to some extent be not traditional but invented by poets of the fifth century or even earlier. On the other hand, Comedy did not come into being simultaneously with official recognition. Aristotle knew, or guessed, that previously there had been plays presented by private enterprise and that these already had characteristic forms. But what these were he does not say (*Poetics* 1449 b 1–3).

He seems to have looked for the origins of Athenian comedy in two places, on the one hand in dialogue between the chorus of 'phallic songs' and its leader, on the other in the influence of Sicilian drama, in which he saw the source of 'plot'. He clearly had in mind Epicharmus, who wrote plays in verse for performance in Syracuse towards the end of the sixth century and the beginning of the fifth. There is nothing in the fragmentary remains to suggest that Epicharmus used a chorus except a few plural titles, for example *Persians, Dancers, Citizens, Sirens,* and these may just as well refer to characters in a play. Many of his personages were drawn from mythology: Alcyoneus, Amycus, Busiris, Philoctetes, the Sphinx, etc. Nearly half, perhaps more, were of this kind. Heracles was a character who lent himself to comedy; a hero of great strength must also be a great eater:

> May you die (?) if you should see him eating. There's a roar from his gullet, his jaw clatters, his molars grate, his canines squeak, he whistles through his nostrils, and wobbles his ears (frag. 21).

Other plays were concerned with the life of Epicharmus' own times, as appears from this extract from a play entitled *Hope* (or alternatively *Wealth*); it anticipates Athenian comedy of Aristotle's time in picturing the type of man who was later to be given the name of *parasite*:

> Dining with the man who wants me—he need only invite me—and with the man who don't—I've no need of any invitation. And then I'm witty and cause a lot of laughter and sing the host's praises; and if anyone tries to contradict him, I pitch into the fellow, and that's how I got myself disliked. And then when I've put plenty of food and plenty of drink inside me, I go. There's no slave to carry a torch for me; I creep along, slipping, and all alone in the dark. If I meet the watch, I count it a blessing from heaven that they want nothing more than to use their whips on me. But when I have got home, quite done in, I sleep without blankets; and I don't drop off at once (frag. 35).

Epicharmus was slightly older than the first Athenian writers of comedy whose names are preserved, and he may therefore have exerted an influence upon them. That is all that can be said. There is nothing to confirm a belief that he did affect them.

Aristotle's second source for comedy, namely dialogue between a 'phallic' chorus and its leader, has at least the merit of explaining the large part played by the chorus in Athenian comedy. There were ceremonies in Attica at which a large erect phallus, symbol of fertility, was displayed and songs were sung. The participants themselves did not wear phalli, any more than did the chorusmen of comedy. Such a ceremony is represented in *The Acharnians*, but only incidentally, and it plays no part in any other play. Semus, an author from the island of Delos, writing perhaps in the second century BC, described the entry of phallus-bearers into a theatre (it is not said in what town), where after reciting some verses, they ran forward and jeered at persons they picked on. This reminds one of the large element of mockery in Old Comedy. But there is nothing to show that any 'phallic' choruses ever conducted a dialogue with a leader, or that they ever 'acted', that is to say represented characters not their own. One may suspect that Aristotle, believing tragedy to have arisen from a dialogue between a dithyrambic chorus and its leader, imagined a parallel origin for comedy.

Elsewhere Aristotle reports that the Megarians, both those who shared a frontier with Athens and those of Sicily, claimed to have originated comedy. The latter seem to have asserted that Epicharmus had originally been one of them before moving to Syracuse, and the mainland Megarians certainly had comic performances in his time. One of the slaves whose conversation opens *Wasps* may allude to such when he tells the spectators 'not to expect any laughs stolen from Megara'. Similarly Eupolis wrote: 'Herakles, this mockery of yours is outrageous, Megarian, and quite frigid: as you see, the children are laughing at it.'

To act and to act for laughs is a widespread human activity. Children do it spontaneously. It is *prima facie* likely that some form of comic acting took place in many cities. Even at Sparta 'there was an old manner of comic play . . . a man would represent harvest-thieves or a foreign doctor, using simple ordinary language . . . and those who pursued this sort of game were called *deikelistai* [*deikeliktai* in the local Dorian dialect].' Athenaeus, who reports this, adds that there were similar performers at Sicyon, at Thebes, in Italy, and elsewhere, who had various names, which include 'improvisers' and 'volunteers'. At Sicyon they were 'phallus-bearers', or did the word there mean 'phallus-wearers', to be compared with the actors at Athens? The claim of Megara to be the source of comedy may have rested on the persistence there of a primitive form of drama, whereas at Athens primitive drama had been superseded and forgotten; with the result that the native origin of Athenian comedy was no longer remembered.

The word comedy is in Greek *Kōmoidia*, or *kōmos*-singing. An alternative ancient derivation from *kōmē* 'village' is linguistically false, but it is likely enough that villages knew *kōmoi*, or 'revels'. Revels took the form of dancing, singing and processions; they could be attached to the worship of a god, particularly of Dionysus; they were easily connected with feasting and drinking. Revellers are likely to adopt many varied ways of amusing themselves; it can be fun to go and sing ribaldries outside the house of someone who is unpopular, or to gratify the widespread human desires to imitate and to parody. From such beginnings a plausible origin for comedy can be sought. It would explain the association of singers and dancers with actors and the prominence given to ridicule of individuals.

There is a little evidence from art which may be relevant. Several Athenian vases of the late sixth or early fifth century show a group of men identically disguised, sometimes masked, moving to the music of a piper. They are dressed as birds, or women, or joined in pairs as horses and riders; others are mounted upon dolphins or ostriches, or walk on stilts, wearing Scythian caps. Such disguised groups were probably a feature of some festival or other, and can be seen as forerunners of many choruses of Old Comedy.

4

New Comedy

NEW Comedy is the name we give, adopting the practice of the later ancient critics, to the Greek plays (other than tragedies) written in the period following the death of Alexander the Great. Plays of this genre seem to have had a recognisable basic form, generally accepted by their authors, and reached by a process of development from Old Comedy. They were composed in five acts, divided by interludes irrelevant to the action. These were performed by the chorus which took no part in the play proper. Published texts recorded the presence of these interludes but not their content. The actors' padding and phalli were things of the past; they were now dressed in decent conventional contemporary clothes and represented the men and women, free and slave, whom one might have met in an Athenian street or home. But masks were still worn; those of young men and women were handsome, but those of the elderly and of slaves were grotesque exaggerations of the human features. The stories were mostly set in Athens, because that was the dramatic centre of the Greek world. Playwrights and actors came there from other cities. But the plays they wrote had few references to individual Athenians or to events at Athens. They treated universal, not local, themes and the plots were, by comparison with those of Old Comedy, realistic.

The transition to the new form took place during the first three-quarters of the fourth century, and the plays of that period came to be given the name of Middle Comedy. But they were a very varied lot. It was a time of change and experiment. No firm line can be drawn between Middle Comedy and Old on the one hand or between Middle and New on the other. Of necessity some writers produced plays during more than one period. In fact the only two extant Greek dramas to which the label of Middle Comedy can be attached are by Aristophanes.

These plays, *Women at the Assembly* (392?) and *Plutus* or *Wealth* (388), retain the element of fantasy that was later to disappear; in the former the Athenian women, disguised as men, pack the assembly and pass a resolution to hand over the direction of the country to themselves, whereupon they try to deal with economic problems by ordering the community of property and with sexual ones by giving the oldest women first turn of the men. Neither reform, as may readily be imagined, proves a success. *Plutus* has a happier, although less hilarious, ending; the god of Wealth is cured of his blindness and gives his favours to men according to their deserts. The concern which both these plays show for the poor is no doubt related to economic conditions at Athens, a city which had lost a war and with it an empire. Comedy has not yet abandoned the characteristic of being topical; there are also lines which jeer, somewhat half-heartedly, at individuals, often politicians. Fragments from contemporary writers of comedy show that this interest in politics and personalities was still quite usual. In later times it was not realised that the disappearance of personalities was a gradual process and it was ascribed to some new law. 'Freedom,' wrote Horace, 'slipped into violence, a fault which deserved regulation by law; the law was accepted and the right to injure was removed' (*Ars Poetica* 282–3). Of such a law there is neither record nor trace. Perhaps poets thought it prudent not to attack powerful men who might find some cause for arraigning them in the courts, but the only public action to restrain them was in 439, the time of the revolt of Samos, when a resolution was passed forbidding the ridicule of individuals. It was repealed two years later, the crisis being over. Something similar was attempted in 415, but, if the proposal was passed, it must have been reversed before *Birds* was staged in 414. The right to ridicule and satirise may have been unwelcome to politicians, but it was valued and guarded by the poets and the people.

Comedy in fact never surrendered the right to criticise in this way, although it was exercised less and less as time went on. Menander glanced occasionally in his earliest plays at men who were established butts and in the last decade of the century Philippides dared to write these lines of Stratocles, agent of Demetrius the Besieger of Cities, whose army kept the 'democratic' faction in power:

> He who took the acropolis for an inn and lodged courtesans with the virgin goddess . . . he because of whom the frost nipped our vines, he because of whose impiety the sacred robe was split, when he transferred the gods' honours to a man. This, not our comedy, is what destroys the people.

But Aristophanes' two plays show other features that were new and were to be developed. The language has become more restricted than that of his earlier work; the vocabulary of the streets is giving way to that of literature. Another self-imposed restriction is that the place of the dramatic action no longer shifts with arbitrary freedom. As already in the *Clouds*, the scene is permanently outside houses belonging to characters of the play. This was to become the standard practice, being part of the movement towards naturalism.

In *Women at the Thesmophoria* and *Frogs* the *parabasis* had been truncated; in these plays it has been dropped altogether. It was moreover thought unnecessary to preserve the words of some of the choric songs, which are represented in our manuscripts by the phrase 'Little piece by chorus', or by abbreviation just 'By chorus'. What was sung must have been essentially, perhaps totally, irrelevant to the play. One cannot even be sure that the poet troubled to write any words for these songs; he may have left it to his chorusmen to sing whatever they fancied. This growing irrelevance of the chorus is illustrated by the first songs of *Plutus*, which are quite extraneous and could be sung by any band of revellers. But the verses spoken by the leader of the chorus in these plays, although no longer numerous, are still integrated into the text; the chorus was not yet simply a device, as it was to be in New Comedy, for creating a break in the action.

The plot based on mythology, not uncommon in Old Comedy, became still more popular in Middle Comedy. Aristophanes' last plays (now lost), *Aiolosikon* and *Kōkalos*, which were produced by his son, were of this kind. The former represented Aeolus, king of the winds, as a cook, while the latter seems to have involved the story that Minos of Crete, having pursued Daedalus to the court of Cocalus, king of a town in Sicily, was drowned in a hot bath. But audiences must have come to tire of such burlesques, for to judge by surviving titles, they occurred but rarely among the dramas of New Comedy.

Mythological plays will, however, have had an influence on the development of comedy. Just as the stories of mythology were the subjects of tragedy, travesties of them will have been affected by its structure. Whereas Old Comedy often presented a series of scenes loosely strung together in an arbitrary sequence, tragedy tended towards a more integrated form of plot, in which each incident grew with seeming inevitability out of what had gone before. The humorous treatment of mythological stories no doubt led to the introduction from the comic tradition of scenes unnecessary to the progress of the story, but it is also probable that basically there was an adherence to the tragic pattern. Comedies of this sort, by telling a unified continuous tale, of which the decisive outcome or climax was not reached until the end, will have helped to make this construction popular. The first steps towards it can already be seen in Aristophanes. One may compare *The Acharnians*, where Dikaiopolis obtains and establishes his peace before the *parabasis* and thereafter merely enjoys its blessings, with *Knights*, in which the struggle to free Demos from the clutches of the Paphlagonian (i.e. Cleon) is not resolved until shortly before the end. Again, the early recovery of the goddess in *Peace* can be contrasted with the postponement of a solution until the penultimate scene of *Lysistrata*.

Comedy also profited from tragedy by the borrowing of motifs. Satyrus, the biographer of Euripides, wrote:

> ... confrontations of husband and wife, father and son, slave and master, unexpected reversals of circumstance, raping of virgins, supposititious children, recognitions by means of rings and necklaces; these are, no doubt, the main constituents of the more recent comedy, and it was Euripides who brought them to the highest pitch of development.

By 'more recent comedy' he probably meant all that succeeded Old Comedy. To call these things the 'main constituents', even of New Comedy, is an exaggeration, but they were certainly frequent constituents. It is possible that some of them were first used by way of parody, just as Aristophanes parodied a scene from Euripides' *Telephus* in his *Acharnians*, and were then found convenient for the more realistic and more romantic plots that gradually became established as the norm.

Whereas Plato could still see in comedy an element that excited envy and spite (*Philebus* 51 C), a generation later Aristotle described it as the representation of inferior characters whose ugliness was of a kind to excite laughter rather than distress (*Poetics* 1449 a 32). Plato was of course hostile to drama, while Aristotle examined it with sympathy,[1] but the difference is also significant of a change in comedy's nature during the fourth century. The personal attacks that were once typical of it gave way to caricature of invented personages. A feature of many plays of Middle Comedy was their satire of certain social types that were of growing importance in the fourth century. The most frequently ridiculed were the professional soldier, the professional cook and the independent courtesan. They seem first to have appeared as comic treatments of real living persons, but these were succeeded by fictitious characters who followed those trades.

The employment of mercenary soldiers was increasing, and men whose profession it was to command them attracted attention. The comic poet loved to represent them as vain, boastful and vulgar in their ostentation of wealth newly gained from booty. They could be associated with another stock character, the flatterer or toady, sometimes called 'parasite'. Literally this word meant 'one who feeds alongside', and was the title of certain priests, who shared the meals offered to their gods; it was then applied in jest to persons who obtained their dinners by the bounty of rich patrons whom they served. Not only the toady, but also the courtesan might attach herself to

[1] Unfortunately his detailed treatment of comedy does not survive.

the soldier. She was represented as greedy, unreliable and insincere. The less-demanding soldier might be content with the wares of the owner of slave-prostitutes, a man who belonged to another calling whose followers were despised and disliked.

The cook is the character about whom most is known, because Athenaeus quoted many speeches by cooks in his *Deipnosophists*, or *Learned Men at Dinner*. The ancient Greek did not have a servant who specialised in cooking. His daily food was simple, and when a man who could afford it wanted a more elaborate meal he called in a professional cook. These persons were, in comedy at least, not slaves but self-employed men of low social status. They were obliged to work with slaves, either their own assistants or members of the household where they were employed. Some, if not all, were not of Attic birth and may have come from Asia Minor or Sicily, places of gastronomic renown.

Their characteristics in drama were inquisitiveness, loquacity, and pride in their cuisine. They remained popular with many poets of New Comedy, who allowed long speeches by cooks to hold up the progress of their plots. Aristophanes' plays had often ended with a festive dinner, a fitting climax to a light-hearted story, and this tradition of conviviality lived on. Many plots of New Comedy led up to a marriage and attendant marriage-feast; or if a young man was entangled with a courtesan, he would wish to entertain her. So there was often place for a cook among the dramatis personae.

Many statuettes from the first half of the fourth century represent slaves in actors' costume, masked, padded and phallic—evidence of their increased importance in plays of that period. Aristophanes had not made great use of them, although there are instances foreshadowing what was to come. In *Frogs* the opening scenes are built round the relation between Dionysus and his slave Xanthias, who is put upon but finally turns the tables on his master. In *Plutus* the slave Karion, described by his master as 'most faithful and most thieving', has a larger part than any other of the human characters; the unity of the play depends on him. From such beginnings the role of the comic slave was developed. No doubt there were in real life slaves who cheated their masters and others who exercised influence over them. The audience in the theatre liked to see such things exaggerated; they were entertained by the slave's cunning wiles and the importance he arrogated to himself. Of course not all slaves in drama will have been of this type; there will doubtless have been others more simple-minded to act as foils.

We have now in our mind's eye a set of characters round whom it was possible to construct the plots of plays, the incidents of which, although perhaps unlikely, were not in themselves completely incredible, as were so many in Aristophanic comedy. One such plot is known from the *Persa* or *Persian* of the Latin author Plautus, if as seems likely he adapted it from a Greek drama written when Persia was still an independent country (506 ff.), that is before 334. A slave Toxilus, whose master is abroad, is in love with a girl, Lemniselenis, who is in the hands of a brothel-keeper named Dordalus. Another slave, Sagaristio, whose master has entrusted him with money to purchase oxen, gives it to Toxilus, enabling him to buy her. Meanwhile Toxilus has been planning a stratagem; he persuades a poor parasite, Saturio, to lend him his daughter to be dressed up as an Arabian girl, whom Sagaristio, disguised as a Persian, proceeds to sell to Dordalus, thus recouping the price paid for Lemniselenis. Thereupon Saturio appears and hauls Dordalus off to charge him with the crime of buying a free Athenian. The slaves, joined by Lemniselenis and a third young slave, settle down to drink, invite the discomfited Dordalus to join them, and subject him to verbal insults and physical indignities.

There were probably better plays than this. But it contains elements to be paralleled in other works. A slave carries through a stratagem to obtain money. A 'parasite' acts dishonestly. A foreigner, with the disreputable trade in women, gets into trouble and is humiliated. The hero is left in possession of the woman he loves, who has protested her love for him. The final scene is one of revelry. But no parallel can be adduced for Saturio's daughter who acts her part as a noble Arab captive most plausibly, provided one accepts the Arab's ability to speak a foreign tongue. Such deceit looks unusual in a young Athenian girl; but like father, like daughter.

The plots of New Comedy made much use of motifs and characters which we know to have been introduced by writers of an earlier period. Doubtless there were also novelties, but they did not remain the property of their inventors. Again and again we meet soldiers, flatterers or parasites, courtesans, bawds, slavers and brothel-keepers, cooks and their assistants, young men in love, strict or miserly old men, cunning slaves, loyal slaves, elderly wives, nurses and merchants. Again and again motifs are repeated: rich young men rape poor girls, but obstacles to marrying them are in the end removed; newly born children are exposed if unwanted (this was true to life), and rescued to be brought up by substitute parents, usually of humble station (probably this was of less frequent occurrence); older children are kidnapped by pirates; these exposed or stolen offspring are finally recognised and welcomed back by their true parents; impecunious young men want girls who are in the hands of traders who make or intend to make them prostitutes; slaves help to find the cash needed to buy them by stratagems directed against the owner or against their own master; slaves come running on the stage either in fright or with unexpected news; brides are given handsome dowries. 'Nothing,' wrote the Roman dramatist Terence, 'is said, that has not been said before.'

These are facts that must be faced. Some critics have seen fit to condemn New Comedy as sterile and dreary repetition. They misunderstand the nature of Greek art, which did not seek to impress by shrill novelty and denunciations of the successes of the previous generation, but to discover new ways of treating old themes. One does not complain that houses are so often built of red bricks, tiles, mortar, glass and deal, and wish architects to show originality by using other materials, bricks of plastic, aluminium sheeting, old bottles and balsa wood. The stock motifs had been found useful for the making of comedies and were not abandoned; but the poets tried to use them in new ways and in new combinations, or would sometimes modify them in an unexpected direction. Part of the spectator's pleasure, if he had seen many plays, lay in noticing how traditional features were altered and in recognising allusions to them. But if he were new to the theatre, old themes would be new for him.

Apart from that, these standard elements, only a few of which are found in any one play, form no more than part of its material. In the best work of New Comedy the real concern is with the individuality of the characters, on the one hand, and their relation one to another, and to the evolution of the plot, on the other hand, to be seen as determined by the reactions of these characters to the initial circumstances.

It has already been observed that Greek dramatists liked to associate certain qualities with certain professions or callings. Some remarks made by the novelist Fielding in his own defence are relevant here:

> Thou art to know, friend, that there are certain characteristics in which most individuals of every profession and occupation agree. To be able to preserve these characteristics, and at the same time to diversify their operations, is one talent of a good writer. Again to mark the nice distinction between two persons actuated by the same vice or folly is another; and as this last talent is found in very few writers, so is the true discernment of it found in as few readers (*Tom Jones*, Book X, chap. 1).

The Greek dramatist appears to have been more hopeful of finding true discernment among his spectators; he has not always been treated with it by his modern critics.

It is a remarkable feature of New Comedy that the same name is given to different characters in various plays. Where slaves are concerned this is less surprising, since even in real life there was no great stock of names for them. They were most frequently called after their place of origin, e.g. Syros, 'Syrian', or Getas, from the Thracian tribe the Getae. Thus there was a Daos, whose name indicates a Phrygian background, in at least eight of the seventeen identifiable plays by Menander of which papyrus fragments have been found. It is more remarkable that there is a similar duplication of names for citizens, who in real life used a great variety. The same seventeen plays have four young men called Moschion and three called Gorgias. The former is a 'speaking' name, 'Little Bull-calf', while each Gorgias is a country lad. Similarly more than one old man has the name of Demeas, or Laches, or

Smikrines, the last being given to men who are too much attached to money.

Perhaps these stock names are parallel to the use of stock masks. It would not have been possible to invent a distinctively individual mask for each of the thousands of slaves who were characters in the various comedies of this period. A thousand real men have a thousand different faces, but masks are simplified reproductions of the human face, emphasising certain features. So it was natural, as well as convenient, that certain types of mask, found to be effective, should be used over and over again. The encyclopaedist Pollux describes forty-four types which he assigns some to slaves, some to old men, some to youths and so on. Many of these types can be recognised in statuettes and other artistic representations. Just as the audience knew that a Daos was a slave, they would also recognise the wearer of certain kinds of mask as being a slave, for example if he had receding red hair, a ruddy complexion, a large thick-lipped mouth and a squint. But it may be hasty to suppose that the mask-makers were strictly confined to Pollux's list.

This failure to give individual names may confirm a prejudice that the characters of New Comedy lack individuality, but it will do so unjustly. A name that indicates no more than age or status does not inhibit the dramatist from conceiving the character as an individual personality; and a love of money can take many forms and be combined with a multitude of other traits. Menander's Moschions have little in common beyond sexual experience or appetite. Moschion of *Perikeiromene* (*Shorn Tresses*) is a conceited youngster who fancies himself as a lady-killer, he of *A Samian Woman* is ashamed of himself and eager to marry the girl he has wronged. What is strange is that the writer who conceived these individualised personalities did not give them names of their own. This was not a matter of principle, since sometimes he did use names that were uncommon in real life and so far as we know unique in comedy: Knemon, Kichesias, Thrasonides.

Probably all that can be said is that there was a tendency to give metrically convenient names that had in theatrical tradition become associated with characters of a particular status, old men, or young men, or married women, or nurses, or hetairai. But this was not made into a rule. Some of the unusual names are of themselves suited to their characters: Polemon from *polemos*, 'war', and Stratophanes from *stratos*, 'army', will clearly be soldiers. The name Knemon may have carried some hint that now escapes us, and Kichesias may be intended to refer to his 'hitting on' (*kichein*) his lost daughter. But if these names have an appropriate meaning, they are all taken from life, and to be compared with Fielding's Alworthy rather than with Sheridan's Lady Sneerwell or Ben Jonson's Sir Politick Would-Be.

Many plays of New Comedy had a 'prologue'; perhaps it was usual. This was an address to the audience, which might be spoken by a character in the play, but was more frequently given to a divine figure, this a practice borrowed from tragedy. Its function was to inform the spectators of the situation at the time when the action began. The modern dramatist is obliged to smuggle these facts into his dialogue; some succeed in concealing what they are doing, but there are plays in which long passages stand out as being 'exposition', for the audience's sake, not that of the characters themselves. Because of the tradition in which he wrote, the author of New Comedy had no need to resort to expedients of this kind.

In pantomime today some characters, notably the Dame, openly recognise the presence of the audience; she even calls on it to sing, and may invite children on the stage. In *Peter Pan* they are challenged to shout their belief in fairies. The actors of Greek comedy had a similar relation to their audiences. They accepted their presence and their interest in the events going forward on the stage. There was a strange make-believe involved in this, for no one expected the spectators to intervene, to shout warnings of danger, or to give ill-informed characters facts that would be useful to them. But the actors had to give the spectators the facts they needed to understand the play, and this was done openly and without embarrassment. A man who is in a quandary can simply inform the audience of his difficulty and of his reflections about it. A man who has failed in an errand will just tell the audience on his return how he has failed; the dramatist is not required to bring on the stage someone else to whom he may explain his failure.

That is not to say that dramatists spurned, if it was suitable, the modern method of making a man talk to himself. Sometimes also they wrote speeches that could as well be soliloquy as address to the audience; but it may be suspected that ancient actors preferred to treat them in the second way.

This practice of one-sided conversation with the public made natural the use of the prologue for exposition. That the speaker should represent a divine personage was often necessary. The plot might be such that no character was in possession of all the facts necessary to understand the situation; the discovery of some that were previously unknown could indeed bring the dénouement of the play. But although they were unknown to the characters whose affairs had formed the subject of the play, the prologue had seen to it that they were not hidden from the spectators.

In this must be recognised an important and striking feature of many plays of New Comedy. The dramatist did not use the device of keeping up his sleeve facts with which to surprise the audience. Instead he gave them a share in divine omniscience. They could enjoy their superior knowledge as they understood the misapprehensions and the blindness of the men and women whose fortunes they watched. At the same time they knew that the materials existed, if only they could be assembled, which would secure a happy ending. The fears and distresses which afflicted the characters could win sympathy, to be sure, but had no need to cause anxiety among spectators who knew them to be unfounded.

For not only did they know that a happy ending was possible, but the divine prologue sometimes concluded by promising it. Even if that reassurance had not been given, they had gone to the theatre to watch a comedy, and comedies always turned out happily. One might be uncertain how a 'tragedy' would end; a comedy had to be cheerful; it could not bring final discomfiture or disaster for those characters who had engaged sympathy, although the humiliation of villains would be greeted with pleasure. So by putting his cards on the table, as it were, from the beginning the dramatist did not surrender a major means of suspense. The conclusion could not be in doubt. All that he lost was the power to leave the audience in the dark about a missing piece of the puzzle, and this he was in any case bound to lose with anyone who saw or read the play for a second time. For the loss of this simple one-time effect he gained a rich field for dramatic irony and for contrasts between truth and ignorance or false beliefs, features which give continuing pleasure.

But although the spectator was in no suspense about the result, although he knew that father and child would be re-united, and that the young hero would obtain the girl he loved, he enjoyed another kind of suspense, that of not know-ing how this result would be brought about, what would be the train of events to achieve it. This is another way in which comedy learned from tragedy. Almost everyone in the theatre will have known that Orestes killed his mother and her lover Aegisthus; what excited interest were the steps he took to achieve their deaths. One could not even be certain that his first plan would be successful. In Aeschylus' *Choephoroe* Orestes explains how he expects to gain access to Aegisthus (560–76); in the event nothing goes according to his expectations, but he kills him nevertheless. In their plays entitled *Electra* Soph-ocles and Euripides handled the same story as Aeschylus, but each in his own way. Similarly, if many comedies had a con-clusion which had been prophesied or could be predicted, that did not rob them of interest; the interest lay in seeing how that conclusion would be reached.

The leading dramatists of New Comedy worked in its initial period, about 320 to 280 BC. The Athenian Menander, Diphilus from Sinope on the Black Sea, and Philemon, who was probably a Syracusan, were all writing at this time, and the long-lived Alexis, native of Thurii in southern Italy, who had begun his career about 350, was still active. It is important to recognise that this was not a time of political quiet at Athens, but one of crises and upheaval. Her attempt after the death of Alexander the Great once again to play a leading role in military affairs by uniting Greek resistance to the Macedonians proved a failure, and in 322 she had to surrender unconditionally to Antipater of Macedon. But that did not mean the end of political activity.

Fundamentally the people were divided between those who wished for security, which they expected to maintain by loyal acceptance of Macedonian protection, and those who hoped to regain independence by allying themselves with others among the powers who disputed Alexander's inheritance. The former party had the support of most of the wealthier members of the community, the latter that of the poorer and of the supporters of democracy, or equal rights for all citizens.

At first the presence of a Macedonian garrison at the Peiraeus enforced a revolution which limited the franchise to those who owned property to the value of twenty minae, not a large sum, but one which appears to have excluded more than half the citizens, who were also disbarred from sitting on juries; juries, it must be remembered, decided many cases which had political origins or political objects. There was a brief restoration of democracy in 318, lasting about a year. Ten more years of limited franchise ended in 307, when the democrats, regaining power with the help of Demetrius, Besieger of Cities, son of Antigonus, ruler of Asia Minor, attempted military action against Macedon, first successfully, then disastrously. He rescued them, but later his defeat at Ipsus in 301 led to a pro-Macedonian swing. In 198 he began to interfere again and his opponents began to kill his supporters. Previous changes of power had been marked by the execution, exile, or suicide of prominent leaders. Now there was open civil war: the democrats held the Peiraeus, while the so-called moderates, under dictatorial leadership, supported a long siege in the city, until starved into surrender in 294. But the see-saw between the pro-Macedonian and the nationalist forces, which was also one between rich and poor, continued, not in isolation but in association with the struggle between Alexander's heirs, who now controlled the major military forces. It ended only in 262 when, defeated in the war she had launched by the decree of Chremonides, Athens finally accepted Macedonian dominance and conservative government by men of means.

To these events there are few allusions in New Comedy. Because politics has so little part in the plays, some have supposed that they also had little in most men's lives. That is a hasty conclusion. Menander himself is said narrowly to have escaped death in the revolution of 307, and one of his plays missed performance because the civil war caused the cancellation of the festival at which it would have appeared. Athens was no longer a major power, and the politics of Athens were no longer such as to be of prime interest to the historian of the Greek-speaking world. But they did not lack importance for the Athenians whose lives they determined. They were bitter and sometimes deadly. They were not a suitable subject for entertainment on a holiday. Even Aristophanes had shut his eyes to many unpleasant political facts; the authors of New Comedy shut their eyes, generally speaking, to politics as a whole. In this they did no more than follow a tendency clearly visible from the beginning of the fourth century; poets seem more and more to have found their material in everyday non-political life, and more and more to have eliminated references to active politicians.

The changes of the late fourth century did not, however, leave comedy untouched. The lifting from the rich of the burden of 'liturgies', not reversed by the restored democracy of 307, meant that the chorus was no longer paid for by a private individual; production was put in the hands of a public official, the *agōnothetēs* or 'competition-manager'. It is not known whether this had any consequences for the dramatists. But the cessation of payments from the theoric fund to the disenfranchised probably resulted in the absence from the theatre of the poorer and on the whole simpler and less educated and less critical members of the public. This would encourage the elimination of vulgarity and obscenity in favour of the literary merits which characterise New Comedy.

Having abandoned public affairs, the dramatists turned to the representation of some aspects of private life. The society of which they give a picture is one in which a leading part is played by men of what we today call the higher income groups. They own at least one household slave, frequently several. Often they have a farm, where manual work is socially acceptable; but their main residence is not necessarily on it; the better off will have a house in the city as well. Vaguely described business abroad is another source of income;

journeys to trade or collect debts are convenient motifs to explain the absence from home of the head of the family.

Families are small; there is rarely mention of more than two children, often a boy and a girl. If both parents are still alive, there is frequently friction between them. A girl is brought up in the seclusion of the women's quarters, from which she escapes only to attend religious festivals. She will be given a dowry and married off to a husband chosen for her by her father, who may have her happiness in view or may wish merely to further his own interests.

A son may be required by a strict father to work on the farm, but most seem to lead an idle life about town. They may see a citizen girl at a festival, fall in love at sight, and finally achieve marriage. It is more usual that they associate with a hetaira; this requires money, which may be provided by an indulgent father or deceitfully obtained from a stingy one, with the aid of the slave who is attached to the service of the young master. Between these extremes are young men who form a relation with a citizen girl to whom they have access, either because she has lost her parents and other relatives or because she is the daughter of a poor widow or grass-widow, who is unable to provide the seclusion usual in a richer household and is willing to allow visits by the lover. The young man may doubt that his father would give consent to a marriage with her; consent may have been legally required, and was in any case necessary in practice, since he was financially dependent.

It would be vain to pretend that the society depicted is that of an average Athenian household. But it is a picture of possible and perhaps not altogether unusual households. It is far from a complete picture even of them. It concentrates on activities, aspects, and human relations which had become established as profitable subjects for the dramatist. One must also remember that, although this kind of society is a norm, dramatists may introduce characters who do not conform to it.

Menander is said to have written over a hundred plays; the titles are known of more than 200 by Antiphanes, a writer of the early half of the fourth century. Even if these poets obtained a chorus on every occasion both for the Lenaia and for the Dionysia, it would seem that not half these plays can have been performed there. How is this to be explained? Some of the titles may have been alternatives, and occasionally a poet may have succeeded in having two plays accepted for one festival, as Anaxandrides did in 375 and Diodorus in 286, but these possibilities are not enough to solve the problem. It is not likely that anyone wrote comedies for no purpose but that of selling the text to a bookseller. Accordingly it is probable that plays were written in the hope of having them produced on some other occasion than those of the great Athenian festivals.

One possibility is that they were intended for other towns, which had built themselves theatres but lacked local dramatic talent; the great theatre at Megalopolis, dating from about 350, and the magnificent one at Epidaurus, constructed about 330, must have been designed for full-scale developed drama, which those places would have been obliged to import. Another outlet for the dramatists may have been the local festivals in Attica, where several of the country *demes* or villages possessed theatres by the end of the fourth century.

Information is scanty, but in some of these places plays were probably to be seen already in the fifth century. An inscription at Eleusis strongly suggests that both Sophocles and Aristophanes produced plays there. Were these first performances or revivals? And if they were first performances, were they later repeated at one of the city festivals? Unfortunately the questions cannot be answered, but there is no *a priori* reason why some plays should not have been performed in the country, but never in the city.

There is evidence for the performance of comedies at seven places in Attica outside Athens. The actors were probably paid professionals, but the chorus may have been composed of amateurs. As at Athens, the plays were in competition; the contest was organised by the *demarch*, or elected headman of the village, and the choruses were assembled and trained by *choregoi*. As at Athens, there were prizes and seats of honour. At the Peiraeus a contractor who provided seating kept the entrance-fees in the early fourth century; at Acharnae towards the end of it they seem to have gone to the *deme*. It would not be surprising if new plays were sometimes written for these elaborately organised festivals.

In Athens itself New Comedy was produced in a reconstruction of the old theatre, carried out under the influence of Lycurgus, a leading political figure, between 336 and 326, a period when Macedonian ascendancy inhibited military expenditure. Permanent stone seating was installed and the stage building replaced by one in stone. There were now without a doubt three doors in it, opening on a stage a few feet above the orchestra and about 66 feet in length. At each end an open pillared building projected from the back wall, enclosing the acting area; through these structures actors could reach the stage from the *parodoi*.[1] Most comedies required the use of two of the doors to represent the entrance to two houses; the third door might be covered, if it was not needed as the entrance to a cave or temple or conceivably a third house. Modern notions of symmetry cause some scholars to assume that when there were two houses the two side doors were used; for what it is worth the ancient evidence states that the larger central door was used for the house of the 'protagonist' or leading actor (Pollux 4. 124).

In some towns soon after Lycurgus' time theatres were built on a different plan, to which his theatre was later adapted. The stage was for some reason unknown raised to the level of the upper storey of the two-floored stage-building and supported on columns which stood in front of the lower storey. It seems, sometimes at least, to have been protected by a projecting roof. The chorus may have remained in the orchestra, its irrelevance to contemporary plays symbolised by its separation from the actors; yet, reduced to a handful of members, it may have performed like them on the elevated stage.

It seems that scene-painting, in the modern sense of the word, was introduced during the period of the elevated stage. Large painted panels were placed between the doors which opened on it, with different sets for tragedy and comedy. It may be relevant that the 66-foot width of the stage could be

[1] These structures must have obstructed the view of some parts of the stage from the ends of the auditorium. This suggests that the full capacity of the theatre, estimated at 17,000, was not needed for dramatic performances.

extended in imagination. The doors were those of houses to be thought of as opening on a street in a town, a lane in a village, or an open space in the country. Occasionally there was also a temple or the mouth of a cave. The houses or other places were to be imagined as near one another, but not necessarily cheek by jowl. The scenery between the doors would give a suggestion of distance between them.

To match this elasticity of space there was a limited elasticity of time. A longer period must often be supposed to elapse during the interval between acts than was in fact taken up by the performance of the chorus. But it was unusual for the action of the play to exceed the time between dawn and nightfall; the words often call attention to how much has been done, or must be done, in one day.

Inscriptional evidence shows that dramatic contests continued at Athens both for comic poets and for comic actors until 143 BC at least; they may have been ended only by Sulla's sack of the city in 86. One may doubt whether many of the later dramatists, none of whom won any great reputation, did much more than rework traditional elements. That seems to be true of Apollodorus of Carystus, who wrote the originals of Terence's *Phormio* and *Hecyra*.

The popularity of comedy is attested by the fact that in the late third century the number of new plays at the Dionysia was increased from five to six. One old comedy was also regularly revived, not in competition with the new; the first occasion was in 339, and from 311 when *The Treasure* by Anaxandrides, a poet of the Middle Comedy, was presented, it was the customary procedure. In one year about the middle of the third century there was even a contest for old comedies, won by a drama of Diphilus, with one of Menander's in second place.

But in the mid-second century it became impossible to carry out the full programme annually; on the average in half of the years no contest took place at the Dionysia. This heralds the virtual end of new work in comedy; very few names are preserved of writers active in the first century, and of almost none in the Christian era. Yet the playing of old comedies was not extinct; Menander's *Theophorumene* was probably to be seen in the theatre of Dionysus as late as AD 267.

Athens was not the only place to know dramatic contests. Whether evidence of them survives is very much a matter of accident and a record of a competition between tragedies need not mean that there was one for comedies also. But, to confine the list to certainties, comedies are known to have been in competition at more than a dozen places, including Delphi (from about 275 until the first century BC), Delos (284–170), Samos (second century), and the Boeotian town of Orchomenos (first century). Performances by comic actors are recorded at several other cities without explicit mention of a competition. Plutarch's question: 'Why should an educated man go to the theatre except to see Menander?' implies opportunities for seeing his plays in the latter part of the first century AD. In the middle of the second century AD Aelius Aristides deprecates in an address to the people of Ephesus their practice of allowing actors to ridicule individual members of their community. He had a capacity for avoiding hard facts, but makes it appear that topical references were there inserted into comedies, new or old.

This widespread and continued dramatic activity, 'the most popular and influential form of culture for several hundred years',[1] was associated with the rise of guilds of theatre per-

---

[1] A. W. Pickard-Cambridge, *The Dramatic Festivals of Athens*, 2nd edn., p. 241. Numerous fragments of papyrus rolls or codices, i.e. books with leaves, found in Egypt, show that Menander was widely read there until the fifth century or even later. It is remarkable that many texts paid little attention to the reader's convenience. Stage directions were rarely given; an initial list of dramatis personae was far from universal and, what is more surprising, the practice of inserting the names of speakers made slow progress. This is first known from a manuscript not earlier than the end of the first century AD, but although it becomes more common and more systematic as time goes on, the old way also persisted of doing no more to indicate a change of speaker than the placing of a short line, which projected into the margin, below the initial letters of the verse in which or at the end of which the change occurred and a pair of dots (:) where it occurred. Some texts do not have the dots, but only a small space. No wonder that Dion of Prusa (early second

sonnel, who called themselves Artists of Dionysus, and who are often known to have provided the performers for various festivals. The most important of these guilds were the Athenian and the Isthmian–Nemean, rivals formed in the first quarter of the third century, and the Ionian–Hellespontine, which arose later in that century. There were also minor guilds elsewhere. Membership was not confined to actors, but included poets and chorusmen, harpists and pipers, trainers and costumiers; their activities were not restricted to drama, but extended to all the musical events of the festivals.

These guilds were important and respected institutions. Their members were granted such privileges as exemption from taxation and from liability to military service. Their priests, who were chosen from their own number, were about 125 BC given the right to wear golden chaplets and purple robes in all cities. The Roman Senate intervened in their disputes. For their own part they fined members who refused to perform where the guild directed them or to keep their engagements. Later the separate guilds appear to have combined to create a single 'world-wide' organisation, first heard of in a letter of AD 43 from the emperor Claudius, which shows however that it was already recognised by Augustus. It was still active as late as the time of Diocletian (285–305) who, to prevent tax-evasion through the buying by rich men of nominal membership, restricted exemption to true professionals.

---

century AD), when recommending an ambitious man to study Menander, advises him not to try to read the plays himself but to have them acted for him and so avoid the preoccupation involved in reading (18.6).

5

Menander

LATER generations had no doubt that Menander was the greatest writer of New Comedy and condemned the taste of his contemporaries; he was awarded the first prize eight times only. Perhaps the broader strokes of Diphilus from Sinope and Philemon from Syracuse, whom later critics joined with him to constitute a leading trio in this form of comedy, made a greater appeal to the mass audience. Yet there is no evidence that these poets won any more victories than he did; they are credited with no more than three apiece at the Lenaia.[1] Nor is there any record of how often he competed; one cannot assume that his plays were always chosen by the archon for production on the occasions, about fifty in number, when he was theoretically eligible. Artistic merit may not have been the sole consideration which guided that official's choice.

It is known, however, that the judges placed him fifth and last at the Dionysia of 312 and 311, and these are decisions which one suspects it would be hard to defend. A great artist is not necessarily under-estimated in his own lifetime, so that one is encouraged to speculate on the causes of Menander's inadequate success. Possibly his friendship with Demetrius of Phalerum, the unpopular 'Supervisor of the City', imposed by the Macedonians from 319 to 307, created prejudice against his plays. It may be more likely that they suffered because their merits do not all appear at first sight.

A well-known anecdote gives Menander's answer to a friend who expressed surprise that although the Dionysia were approaching he had not written his comedy. 'Indeed I have composed my comedy! The plot is worked out, but I have to add the spell of the verses.' This reply is not to be regarded as a depreciation of the words of the play; they are spoken of as if they were an incantation to charm the hearer.

[1] *I.G.* ii². 2325 col. x.

Menander did in fact write with superb skill, which can unfortunately be appreciated only by those able to read the original Greek. He subtly varied his speed and his rhythms and the levels of his language to correspond with the psychology of his characters and their emotional changes. And although he constantly used the verse form to reinforce the meaning, he maintained the illusion that they were speaking as men speak in reality, colloquially and individually; they do not fall, as Philemon's personages seem to have done, into literary Greek, unless of deliberate purpose. This is even to some extent true of his trochaic tetrameters, although these tend to a more regular movement than the commoner iambic trimeters. But the excellence of the writing need not imply that composition was a slow affair. It may be that he was one of those authors from whom there comes a spontaneous and easy flow of admirable language.

What the anecdote does convey is the primary importance of plot. This does not mean simply the events. Of far more weight are the means by which those events are brought about; they include the psychology of the persons in the play, since the way in which they choose to act determines its course. Hence the imaginative creation of characters is part of the playwright's business, and at this too Menander was outstanding. His people are credible, consistent and lifelike; their emotions and thoughts are often not explicitly expressed but to be inferred from the clues given by their words; and the words are rich in suggestion. The action is then carried forward by doings and speeches suitable to the characters thus depicted.

A good plot gives further pleasure by its formal merits, that is to say by contrasts between successive scenes or between characters and pairs of characters, by symmetry and by mirror-image, by the balanced proportion of the parts. These must not be obtrusive, or they will appear contrived. Analysis of Menander's plays brings many instances of such elegance to light. One difficulty in constructing a plot is to provide natural exits and entrances, as some dramatists have confessed. In Menander they are always plausible. The *moment* at which a character enters or leaves is of course determined by the dramatist, but the *motive* is rarely in doubt or, if not explicitly indicated, can be surmised. Movements are natural reactions to the situation which has arisen by the development of the plot. There are no extraneous, arbitrary factors, like the famous bear which causes Autolycus' exit in *The Winter's Tale*. The difficulty involved in so contriving the progress of the play must have been greatly increased if Menander was under the handicap of having to employ no more than three actors. This is a question on which there is no agreement.

In no surviving scene do more than three characters speak, although sometimes one or more others, who have spoken elsewhere, are on the stage. These silent characters were played by 'supers', who wore the masks that had previously been worn by actors. This restriction to three speakers appears also in the plays by Menander which Plautus adapted, and may have applied to those adapted by Terence; the changes, however, which the latter introduced are too much disputed to allow him to provide unchallenged evidence. The restriction has been explained by some scholars as self-imposed and due either to the difficulty, which can surely be exaggerated, of writing four-part dialogue or to that of recognising in a great open-air theatre which of a number of masked actors was speaking or to an artistic preference for simplicity.

The last explanation is the most difficult to combat, for its supposition that Menander would have found that four speakers offended against his aesthetic sensibility must be intuitively accepted or rejected; it cannot be usefully discussed. Masks certainly prevented the lips from providing any clue to the speaker, but gesture may often have accompanied words, as it does today more usually among southern peoples than with us, and so have served as an indication. If this was so, to pick out the right speaker would not be significantly more difficult if the choice were between four characters rather than three, particularly if the four were divided into pairs, perhaps at opposite ends of the stage, each pair engaged in its own conversation. But there is no such scene. It may also be observed that there is no scene where one of three characters who have been in conversation departs and is immediately replaced by a fourth; yet such a scene would never require the audience to discriminate between more than three actors at once.

The most obvious explanation of the absence of more than three speaking actors from any scene is that Menander wrote so that he could be performed by a company of three actors. It is known that companies who visited Delphi in the third century were so composed; they had three comic actors, five or seven chorusmen and a piper. He may have had such troupes in mind, although it is only a guess that they existed in his time. But he fashioned many of his plays for a première at one of the great Athenian festivals and it is possible that the same limitation was in force there. The travelling companies may have had three actors because that was the number engaged in the original performance.

It is generally agreed that tragedy was performed by three actors: Aristotle is the explicit authority for that and it is confirmed in various ways. On the other hand some plays of Aristophanes require a minimum of five. But did comedy come to accept the limitation traditional in tragedy? It is possible that such a rule was introduced in order to equalise conditions for the competitors; no dramatist was to gain an advantage by being able to employ a larger number of actors. The principal actor, assigned to the author by lot, was paid from state funds and probably used them to hire his assistants. It may have been thought fair that a rich actor or rich author should not be allowed to exceed a standard provision.

This, it must be confessed, is speculation. But if plays were written so that they could be performed by three actors, we have an explanation of the way in which certain exits are managed. For example, in *Dyskolos* (*The Curmudgeon*) Daos does not accompany his master Gorgias and Sostratos to the fields, but goes off first, telling them to follow. This is in character; he is a hard worker and wants to get to his labours. But it does not advance the action. The actor, however, is needed to return shortly as Sikon. Then Sostratos does not go off with Gorgias, but hangs back and talks to the audience. That is because Gorgias' actor must also play Getas, Sikon's companion; he is given time to return in his new role, because Getas is found to have fallen behind under the weight of the baggage he carries. In the *Sikyonios* Theron goes in to tell Stratophanes that the father of the girl the other loves has been found but, although an inquisitive man, does not come back with him. The actor was needed to play Stratophanes himself.

A limitation of actors to three was feasible only if parts were sometimes shared, if for example in *Samia* (*The Woman from Samos*) the part of Parmenon was taken by one actor in Acts I and V and by another in Act III. In a completely realistic theatre this would be impossible, but the theatre of Menander was not of that sort. The fact that the actors were masked is enough to show that the audience looked for no more than a limited realism. By wearing A's mask an actor would become A, for it was by mask rather than voice or stature that A was recognised.

Apart from that, any offence caused by discrepancies between actors playing the same man could be minimised, if it was thought desirable. Notably tall or notably short men may have been regarded as unsuitable for the profession of acting. The art of mimicry, today somewhat out of fashion, which effects the disguise of one's own voice, must have been used by the ancient actor if he distinguished the voices of the different persons he represented in the same play; the same art could have been called upon by the different actors who played a single part; they could both or all three speak in a similar way, just as they could also assimilate their movements and gestures.

In conclusion it must be emphasised that the case for a limitation of actors to three is not cogent. The fact that a play could be performed by three actors does not prove that it was so performed. And even if it was a rule kept at Athens, it may not have been operative in some other place, or even enforced without exception at the Athenian festivals. The find of a new papyrus might establish a breach of the rule, and there are two or three Latin plays, adapted from Diphilus and Apollodorus, in which no simple change suffices to re-establish it.

In those plays, more than a dozen in number, where one can judge, it is either certain or highly probable that Menander used the five-act structure with an expository prologue. The

1a. Actors from a Middle
Comedy (c. 370 B.C.)
*Terracottas from an Athenian
grave.*

1b. Athenian theatre ticket
of lead, inscribed
Theophoroumene (*The Woman
Possessed*). Perhaps third
century A.D.

while his Muse or Comedy stands by.

scarcity of information about Middle Comedy makes it impossible to decide whether these were already established and regularly used conventions or whether his example confirmed what had previously been experimental. But in any case here as elsewhere he must be seen as the inheritor of a tradition within which he worked but within which he created novelty. It may have been on his own initiative that in several plays he gave a surprising place to the 'prologue', putting it after an opening dialogue; surprising, but effective. The audience's attention was immediately gripped by a striking scene, which partially revealed the situation with which the play began, but which was also designed to mislead. It showed the circumstances as they appeared to one or more of the characters. But they were ignorant of some pertinent fact, recognition of which would work a complete change in the spectator's response to what he had seen. The divinity who speaks the prologue is better informed and able to put him right.

In the opening scene of *Aspis* (*The Shield*) the slave Daos reports the death on a campaign of his young master, whose avaricious uncle fails to conceal an interest in his very considerable booty. Then the goddess of Luck, the speaker of the 'prologue', not only spells out the family relationships, and explains the uncle's plans to acquire the dead nephew's estate by exercising a legal right to marry his sister, although another wedding for her was imminent, but also reveals that the young man is in fact alive and, having been taken prisoner, is on the point of returning home; all the miser's efforts will be trouble wasted.

Similarly in *Perikeiromene* (*Shorn Tresses*) the 'prologue' is postponed. The opening scene does not survive, but can be reconstructed in outline with fair certainty. A soldier, returning from an expedition, was met by his servant who had gone ahead; he reported that he had surprised the girl with whom the soldier lived allowing herself to be kissed and hugged by a young man on her doorstep. In a fury of jealousy the soldier hacked off her long hair. The goddess Misapprehension then puts a different face on the affair. The girl knew the young man to be her brother, although he was ignorant of the fact. There is an explanation of how they had come to meet and why she could not reveal their relationship. Finally there is a promise that they will find the family to which they belong and that good will come of the present imbroglio.

Menander was not slow to make use of the traditional figures caricatured in Middle Comedy, soldiers, courtesans, cooks and so on. But he was not content simply to repeat their traditional qualities; when he used old themes he made them a part only of an individual character, or he modified them; sometimes he even contradicted tradition, to create an effect by the unexpectedness of his treatment.

The cook had been inquisitive, talkative and self-important. Sikon in *Dyskolos* shows curiosity as he questions Getas on his mistress's dream; he is not long-winded, but he talks to himself, using a vocabulary rich in oaths and in metaphors; he boasts, not of his cuisine, but of his large clientele and his technique in borrowing utensils; his conceit is shown by his reaction to Knemon's falling into the well:

> Now the Nymphs have given him the punishment he deserves on my account. No one who wrongs a cook ever gets off unscathed. Our art has something sacred about it.

By contrast the cook in *Aspis*, who is seen leaving, not as usual entering, his place of employment, complains that things always go wrong for him. The cook in *Samia* enters in full flow of talk and questions, but is cut short. Later he tries with officious benevolence to interfere as Demeas turns Chrysis out of his house. All these cooks display or contradict traditional characters, but they do it briefly and in sentences woven into the texture of plot and dialogue.

The stupidity, arrogance and vulgarity of the professional soldier, together with his habit of romancing about his exploits, were certainly all displayed in Bias of *Kolax* (*The Flatterer*), the origin of Terence's Thraso in *Eunuchus*. But the three soldiers who appear in the partially surviving plays are sympathetically drawn. Thrasonides of *Misumenos* (*Hated*), wild with love for the captive girl within his power, not laying a hand on her when she shows her repulsion, and generously freeing her without ransom when her father appears, is the hero of the play. Yet he had talked of his exploits, a traditional motif, but it may be guessed, one made essential to the play, for it will have been one of these tales which made the girl suspect him of having killed her brother. Nor is there any reason to think that he exaggerated, for the prologue told that he had served with distinction.

There is no sign of any of the traditional defects in Stratophanes of *Sikyonios (The Man from Sikyon)*. On the contrary his actions are practical and decisive, nor does he forget, at the moment when he seems about to secure the girl he loves, to issue orders for the quartering of the men for whom he is responsible. One can believe that he was a good officer. Polemon, on the other hand, in *Perikeiromene* displays neither the traditional qualities of the caricatured soldier nor those that are required in the field. He is hasty, uncertain of himself and impulsive, but he attracts sympathy by his bewilderment at the situation he has created by the outrage on the mistress he loves, his despair at the prospect of her leaving him, and his pleasure at her discovery of her father.

Similarly the selfish, acquisitive, lying and faithless courtesan, although no doubt a common figure in real life, was not according to Menander the sole type to be found in her profession. He brought into his plays a wide range of hetairai. Habrotonon in *Epitrepontes (The Arbitrants)* is still quite young and still a slave; clever and good-natured, but ready to deceive, not merely to help others but also in the hope of winning her own freedom by the trickery. Chrysis in *Samia* is older and attached to the child she passes off as her own; her lie is told with the best of intentions but infringes the loyalty she otherwise shows towards the man who is keeping her. For others we must go to Latin adaptations. Bacchis of *Heautontimorumenos (The Man Who Punished Himself)* is an unprincipled gold-digger, but Thais of *Eunuchus* acts with dignity when imposed upon and apparently thwarted in her sustained effort to return Pamphila unharmed to her family. To be sure her motives are not purely altruistic, she hopes to secure their friendship and protection. But Menander's world, like the real world, is not one of people blind to their own interests.

He was not the first to abandon the stereotype of the wicked hetaira. Already Antiphanes had written:

> The man of whom I speak saw a hetaira who lived next door to him and fell in love with her. She was of citizen birth, but without guardian or relatives, and had a character of gold for goodness—a true 'companion'.[1] Other women damage that name, really a fine one, by their behaviour.

The innovation is here excused by the woman's citizen birth; Menander extended his sympathy more widely. Yet he followed what seems to have been a rule in New Comedy: a girl of citizen birth must either remain a virgin before marriage, or be faithful to her first lover and marry him when marriage becomes possible.

Menander is also remarkable for presenting a great range of individualised and sympathetically treated slaves; he thought of them neither as mere instruments of their masters' wishes nor as vehicles for comic interludes; they act with their own motivation within a framework provided by the actions, characters, and intentions of their owners; they affect what happens, but do not direct it. This, it may be supposed, does not misrepresent the situation in many Athenian households.

This method of writing, which gives large parts to slaves and develops their personalities on much the same scale as those of their masters, is a testimonial to Menander's range of interest and sympathy: he did not regard slaves as a different kind of creature from the free; all men were human beings and he would give any man the artist's attention. He can fairly be contrasted with many dramatists of the Western world, in whose plays about households of the employing classes servants usually have a quite subsidiary role. Exceptions like Barrie's *Admirable Crichton* and Beaumarchais' *Figaro* were protests against the view that all members of the lower orders are inferior beings, but these characters are not made typical representatives of their status: they are exceptions and remain exceptional.

---

[1] 'Companion' is the literal meaning of the word 'hetaira'.

MENANDER

The recent discoveries which have enriched knowledge of
Menander have made it more and more difficult to generalise
about him in an absolute manner. His plays are like a large
family of brothers and sisters, all recognisable as his work,
each sharing features with some of the others, but each
individually characterised. Plutarch, however, saw in them
one common element, *Eros*, love. The Greek word overlaps
the English, but does not coincide with it. It has a stronger
association with sexual passion and desire, and is sometimes
nothing more than these things. But it easily becomes allied
with more altruistic urges, respect, loyalty, generosity, a wish
for the welfare of the beloved. 'I know,' says Kallippides in
Dyskolos, 'that what gives a young man's marriage security
is that Eros prompted him to it.'

Yet although Eros is a force in all the plays, it is, usually at
least, not their principal subject. As a main interest it would
have been narrow and constricting for the dramatist, who
would have been further limited by the social customs of his
time, which almost entirely prevented contact between young
men and marriageable girls. Eros often sets a play in motion,
for example, *Dyskolos*, *Perikeiromene*, or *Samia*, but it is not
necessarily even the initiating cause. In *Aspis* that is the avarice
of Smikrines, which is then resisted because of its threat to the
eros of Chaireas.

The major subject of *Dyskolos* is the misanthropy of Knemon,
which is shown to be disadvantageous to himself as well as to
others; a minor subject is the desirability of friendship between
rich and poor, and the reciprocal aid they can give one to the
other. In *Samia* the recurring theme is the relation between
father and son, the strains to which it is subjected and its final
survival. *Adelphoi B*, so called to distinguish it, since two of
Menander's plays had the title *Adelphoi* (*Brothers*), the origin
of Terence's *Adelphoe*, is another play in which much attention
is given to the problem of relations between father and son
and in which alternative methods of upbringing are contrasted.
Epitrepontes is a play of extraordinarily rich content; its varied
scenes are developed for their own sakes, yet this threat to the
unity of action is nullified by their skilful attachment to the
central situation, the difficulty that has arisen between Charisios
and his wife. He has found that she had been pregnant when

he married her and had in his absence exposed the child. He has then retreated into a friend's house and hired a hetaira, perhaps with the object of causing his wife to divorce him; thus their marriage would be ended but her good name protected. Her father, who knows nothing of the child, urges this course on her but, in a lost scene which Charisios overhears, she refuses. He has previously learned that he had himself before marriage got a child by rape at a festival and he comes to feel how despicable is his conduct towards his wife, and is convinced that he must hold to her. Only when he has had this change of heart does it come to light that she had been the victim of his rape and that the child, which had been rescued, was theirs. Charisios is on the stage for a mere eighty lines at the end of Act IV, yet the whole of the play revolves around him and the theme of loyalty in marriage.

Yet the importance in some plays of themes which transcend the particular interests of the individuals who illustrate them must not tempt us to look for them everywhere. Menander was a dramatist, not a sociologist. His first concern was to write entertaining plays with a good story, like *Synaristosal (A Women's Lunch-party)* or *Dis Exapaton (A Double Deceit)*, the originals of Plautus' *Cistellaria (A Little Box)* and *Bacchides (The Bacchis Sisters)*.

There are many different ways of writing an entertaining play and there is considerable variety of form in Menander. *Sikyonios* seems to be almost entirely serious, an exciting drama full of incident and rising at times to a style more elevated than was common in comedy. In *Perikeiromene* the scene in which the father recognises his long-lost daughter is composed in stichomythia, or alternate lines, intended at once to be a mark of their emotion and a source of amusement by its borrowing of phrases from tragedy. In neither of these plays is there anything to excite sustained laughter, like Daos' deliberately absurd quotations from tragedy in *Aspis*.

Samia has only six characters, of whom one has no effect on the plot; *Synaristosai* seems to have had eleven, not counting the god who spoke the prologue, and six of them were women, who dominated the play, which is in that respect unique. Some plays reach as early as the fourth act a point where the satisfaction of Eros seems assured; the early *Dyskolos* and the late *Epitrepontes* are examples of this. Thereafter there are scenes which carry on other themes and which conclude with hilarity. But in *Misumenos* and *Sikyonios* the happy ending for the lover is postponed until very near the termination of the play and there is no sign of a conclusion which gave cause for laughter.

This variety may lead one to wonder whether Plautus' *Stichus* has a closer relation to Menander's *Adelphoi A*, alleged to be its original, than most scholars have thought. It is a play almost without plot, consisting of eight scenes or sketches, very tenuously connected. Yet these scenes are clearly divided into five acts, which suggests that Plautus, who wrote for continuous performance, derived them from his Greek original. If so, Menander may for some reason, haste or experiment, have abandoned his usual care for the construction of a plot.

Impossible though it is to find a 'typical' play by Menander, *Samia* may serve as an example of the kind of thing to be expected in his writing. The following account of that play, being largely a summary, can provide only a diminished idea of its merits; even passages of translation can do no more than give the basic sense of the words; they cannot reproduce the skill of the versification. Even if a rendering in verse had been attempted, it must have been inadequate. Blank verse is the only possible form to represent the Greek iambic trimeter but, in comparison, it has few rules.

Samia has no need of a god to let the audience into secrets not known to the human characters; for there are none. A nearly complete explanation of the background is given in an opening monologue by the young Moschion. He has no hesitation about accepting the spectators' presence, but without ado tells them that (he is an adopted child of a rich father),[1] brought up in style and able to help poorer friends. Demeas, his father, had made him a full human being and he

---

[1] There are some lacunae in the text as it survives. I use brackets to enclose matter which may be guessed to have stood in them.

had responded by being well-behaved. Then his father had been taken by desire for a woman from Samos, a hetaira, and ashamed of this passion had tried to conceal it. Moschion had however become aware of it and seen that his father would have trouble from young rivals unless he got the woman under his own control. (So he encouraged him to establish the woman, whose name was Chrysis, in his house. Demeas had left her there when he had gone abroad with their neighbour, a poor man called Nikeratos. Nikeratos had a daughter in her teens and a wife who became friendly with the Samian woman.)

> Running down from our farm, [continues Moschion] I found them all collected in our house with some other women to celebrate the feast of Adonis ... Their noise made it difficult to sleep: they were taking plants up on the roof, and dancing, and making a night of it, scattered through the house. I hesitate to go on with the story, although perhaps it does no good to be ashamed. All the same I am ashamed. The girl became pregnant. By telling you that I make it clear what happened. I was to blame and I did not deny it. I went to the girl's mother of my own accord and promised marriage as soon as my father should return; I swore a solemn oath. When the child was born, I took charge of it, not so long ago. By a lucky chance it happened that Chrysis (had a little earlier given birth to a child who had died; she took the girl's baby in substitution, and so we were able to keep it.

Moschion then left and Chrysis came out of the house; she shortly) sees Moschion returning with their slave Parmenon, whom he seems to have met by accident. Parmenon tells him that he has seen Demeas and Nikeratos; they are back from their travels; Moschion must be brave and raise the question of his marriage at once. 'How? I am turning coward now that the moment comes; I am ashamed to face my father.' 'And what of the girl you have wronged and her mother?' Chrysis makes her presence known, and while Parmenon explains his own reasons for wanting the marriage to take place, Moschion pulls himself together and promises to keep his oath. They confirm the plan that Chrysis should say that she is the child's mother. Demeas will be angry,[1] says Moschion, but she is confident that he will soon get over that; he's enamoured of her, and she will do anything to prevent the child's being put out to nurse in some tenement. (Parmenon and she enter the house, while) Moschion goes off to some quiet place to practise what he will have to say in the coming interview with his father. The stage is empty. There enter Demeas, Nikeratos and slaves with their luggage. They talk about the pleasure of being home again in Athens; Byzantium and the Black Sea were terrible places.

> *Nikeratos.* What surprised me most about that region, Demeas, was that sometimes one could not see the sun for days on end. It seemed as if a thick mist obscured it.
> *Demeas.* No; old Sun could see nothing worth looking at there, and so he gave the inhabitants of those parts just the minimum of sunshine.
> *Nikeratos.* By Dionysus, you are right.
> *Demeas.* Well, we'll let other people bother about that. Now what do you think should be done with regard to that matter we were talking about?

Demeas of course does not believe in his own anthropomorphic meteorology, but amuses himself by passing it off on Nikeratos, whose simplicity is thereby immediately indicated at his first appearance. The passage also prepares the way for a similar move, but in a serious situation, at the end of Act IV. But all this travel talk is primarily designed to form the background from which will suddenly spring the answer to that last question.

> *Nikeratos.* You mean our talk about your boy's marriage?
> *Demeas.* Quite.
> *Nikeratos.* My mind's the same. Let us fix a day and hope it turns out well.
> *Demeas.* Is that agreed then?

---

[1] He would not expect her to allow the child to live without his authority. But the time for infanticide is past.

Nikeratos. By me, it is.
Demeas. And by me too; and I thought of it first.

Only one conclusion can be drawn from these exchanges: the two fathers have agreed on a match between their children. The rich Demeas insists that the scheme had originated with himself and tactfully allows his poor friend to feel that it is his consent that is required. Moschion's fears are then groundless. The play seems to be as good as over (as the two fathers enter their houses).

Act II is badly mutilated, but whereas complications might be expected to set in at this point, difficulties seem hardly to have arisen before they were solved, and once again the play seems threatened by a premature end. Moschion, returning from an unsuccessful rehearsal of his confession, meets his father, greets him, and asks what makes him pull a long face. Demeas replies that he seems to have got a wife in his hetaira, who has provided him with a son without his consent; but she can get to hell out of his house, and take the child with her. Moschion protests with some fine sentiments: 'who of us in Heaven's name is legitimate and who a bastard when he's born a man?' (Demeas was quickly persuaded to keep Chrysis and the child supposed to be his, and as quickly discovered to his surprise that Moschion loved the girl intended for him.) He undertakes to ask Nikeratos to agree to the marriage's taking place that very day and, Moschion having retired, hurries his surprised friend into agreement and sends a puzzled Parmenon to fetch a cook and foodstuffs from the market. Nikeratos must go and tell his wife, who is thought likely to make difficulties, before following Parmenon to the market.

Act III. Demeas comes out and in a long speech of over eighty lines tells the audience of an unexpected development, that has left him in a turmoil of doubt. He describes the busy scene in his house as the slaves were in confusion caused by his orders to prepare for the unexpected wedding. The child was pushed out of the way on a couch, where it lay yelling, and the servants were calling for flour, water, olive oil, charcoal. He himself was giving a hand and went into a store-room, and while he was there an old woman, once his slave and Moschion's nurse, came down from the upper floor by a stair which led into the weaving-room from which the store opened, and

> seeing the baby yelling there with no one to pay it any attention, and not knowing that I was at home, thought she could chatter safely: she goes up to it and says the usual stuff: 'Darling child!' and 'What a treasure! But where's mummy?'; she kissed him and walked him up and down. And when he stopped crying she said to herself 'Oh dear me! It's only yesterday that I was nursing Moschion himself and loving him, and he was just like this baby, and now he has already got a child of his own for me to hold'. A girl came running in from outside. 'Wash the baby,' she says to her, 'What's this? Can't you attend to the little one, when his father's getting married?' The other replied quickly: 'How loud you're talking! Master's at home.' 'You don't say! Where?' 'In the store-room', and then with a change of voice 'Mistress is calling you, nurse' and 'Get a move on! Hurry!—He hasn't heard a thing. What luck!' 'Oh dear me!' she said, 'How I chatter!' and took herself off, I don't know where. I emerged from the store exactly in the way I came out here just now, quite quietly, as if I'd heard nothing and noticed nothing, and I saw her, the Samian woman, outside by herself, holding it in her arms and giving it her breast. So one can know that it is hers, but who is its father, is it my child or is it—no, gentlemen, I'm not saying it, I won't suspect it, I'm just putting the facts before you, what I heard with my own ears, and I feel no resentment—not yet. I know that the lad has always been well-behaved and as loyal to me as could be. But on the other hand, when I remember that the woman who talked was his nurse, and that she was speaking behind my back, and then think of the woman who loves it and has insisted on rearing it against my wishes—I am utterly beside myself.

This speech is beautifully constructed. The initial sentences foreshadow some catastrophe, but the vivid details which follow do nothing to elucidate it, until it bursts as unexpectedly on the audience as it had on Demeas himself. Then, ironically, the one thing he believes he knows is exactly where he is wrong. He forces himself to be calm, but his indignation is too strong and finally explodes. This pattern of behaviour will be repeated.

Now he recovers his self-control, as Parmenon comes home from the market with food and a cook, whose loquacity the slave checks before taking him indoors. Demeas, who has told him to return, has meanwhile let the audience know that he intends to have the truth out of him and so when he comes out full of self-confidence, giving instructions to Chrysis, they can relish his sudden dismay at Demeas' opening words, 'Listen now, Parmenon, there are many reasons why I don't want to flog you,' followed by a demand to know whose the child is. 'It belongs to Chrysis.' 'And who is the father?' 'You are, so she says.' At this Demeas bursts out that he knows perfectly well that it is Moschion's baby and that Parmenon knows it too. Everybody says so. Parmenon sees no hope of keeping up the pretence and is on the point of explaining everything, but unfortunately begins 'We wanted to keep it quiet'. Demeas supposes him to mean 'keep the liaison of Moschion and Chrysis quiet', and in fury proposes to have him branded [lit. tattooed] on the spot. In terror the slave takes to his heels, leaving Demeas to regain control of himself with a mighty effort. Once again he addresses the audience: Moschion must have been seduced by Chrysis; his eagerness for marriage is not due to his being in love, but to escape from her. His past conduct shows him not to be one to behave immorally and disloyally.

> But the creature's a damnable strumpet. Demeas, you must be a man. Forget your desire for her, put an end to love, and do all you can to keep this unlucky affair hidden, for your son's sake, yes, but throw that beautiful Samian head first out of your house and let her go to hell. You have your excuse, that she kept the child. Give no sign that there is anything else; bite your lip and bear it; be brave and see it out.

The cook comes out to look for the missing Parmenon; Demeas pushes past him with a cry of 'Get out of the way!'.

The cook, bewildered, hears shouting inside, and then Chrysis emerges, carrying the baby and followed by Demeas. With violent language he turns her away; twice he is on the point of letting the true reason slip, but checks himself. She of course cannot understand this sudden rage, and well-intentioned attempts on the part of the cook to interfere give a comic condiment to this tragic scene. Finally Demeas re-enters the house and locks the door. Nikeratos, returning from market with a skinny sheep, about which he makes wry jokes, makes a striking contrast to the weeping Chrysis. But when he sees her and learns of Demeas' conduct, he takes her in to his wife.

Act IV. Nikeratos comes out, angry at the lamentations in which the women are indulging, an ill-omen for the wedding: he intends to give Demeas a piece of his mind, but almost immediately meets Moschion, who returning impatient for the wedding learns from him that Chrysis has been turned out because of the baby. Then Demeas emerges and tells the audience that he intends to swallow his anger with Moschion and push on with the marriage. Moschion, who has meanwhile been consulting with Nikeratos, approaches him and a brilliant scene ensues, comic for the audience, grim earnest for the participants. Demeas knows Moschion to be the father, but wishes to conceal his knowledge, Moschion still believes Demeas to think the child his own and Chrysis to be the mother.

Moschion. Tell me, why has Chrysis left and gone?

Demeas. (*aside*) She is sending him to treat with me. This is dreadful. (*aloud*) It's none of your business. It's my affair entirely. Stop your nonsense. (*aside*) Yes, dreadful. He's in it with her to injure me.

Moschion. What did you say?

Demeas. (*aside*) Clearly. Why does he approach me on her behalf? He ought to have been glad at what has happened.

Moschion. What do you think your friends will say when they hear of this?

Demeas. I expect my *friends*, Moschion, to—Leave me alone!

Moschion. I should be a coward if I let you have your way.

Demeas. Are you going to stop me?

Moschion. I am.

Demeas. Look, this beats all. This is more dreadful than ever.

Moschion. Yes, it's not right to give way to anger so completely.

Nikeratos. That's well said, Demeas.

Moschion. Nikeratos, go in and tell her to pop out here.

Demeas. Moschion, leave me alone; leave me alone, Moschion. That's the third time I say it. I know everything.

Moschion. What do you mean by everything?

Demeas. Don't talk to me!

Moschion. But I must, father.

Demeas. You must? Am I not to have control of my own affairs?

Moschion. Do me this favour.

Demeas. Favour indeed! You are as good as demanding that I should walk out of my own house and leave it to the pair of you. Let me see your marriage through, let me see the marriage through, if you have any sense.

Moschion. Of course I let you. And I want Chrysis to be there with us.

Demeas. Chrysis!

Moschion. It's mainly for your own sake that I'm pressing you.

Demeas. Isn't this as plain as plain could be? I call on you to witness, Apollo Loxias, here's someone in league with my enemies. Oh! I shall burst.

Moschion. What do you mean?

Demeas. You want me to explain?

Moschion. Certainly.

Demeas. Come over here then.

Moschion. Tell me.

Demeas. I will. (*in a low voice*) The child is yours. I know. I have heard it from Parmenon, who is in your secrets. So don't try your games on me.

Moschion. Then if this baby's mine, what harm is Chrysis doing you? How is she responsible?

Demeas. What! Have you two no scruples?

Moschion. Why shout at me like that?

Demeas. Why shout, you scum? You can ask that? Tell me, you accept the responsibility as yours and dare to look me in the face as you say it? Have you really broken with me completely?

Moschion. I? How?

Demeas. You say 'how?' You think it fit to ask that?

Moschion. Yes. It's not such an awful matter. I imagine, father, that thousands have done what I have done.

Demeas. My God! Your nerve! Look, I ask you here in public: by whom did you get that child? Tell Nikeratos, if you don't think it awful.

Moschion. Oh, but it would really be awful to tell him just straight out. He'll be angry when he gets to know.

Moschion appears to be on the point of being forced to confess that the mother was Nikeratos' daughter, when Nikeratos at last understands Demeas' suspicions and indignantly de- nounces the bewildered boy as a worse criminal than the most famous incestuous figures of mythology, who are for him historical personages. Urging Demeas to revenge, he rushes into his house to turn out the evil woman he finds he is shelter- ing. His absence allows Moschion to attempt to dispel his father's misunderstanding and confess the truth. Demeas remains sceptical, until Nikeratos staggers out alone and in language that would pass in a tragedy announces that he is maddened, struck to the heart by an unexpected cause of woe, and then with a sudden collapse of style that he'd caught his daughter suckling the child. Moschion dare not face him and runs. Demeas plays for time. 'Perhaps she was only pretending.' 'No, she fainted when she saw me.' 'Perhaps she thought——' 'You'll be the end of me with these "perhapses".' 'Well, I don't believe it.' Nikeratos dashes back into his house. Demeas reproaches himself for having caused this crisis; his friend is a man who will stop at nothing. He hears him shouting and threatening to incinerate the child [to get rid of the evidence of his daughter's dishonour].[1] But the next moment Nikeratos is out again. 'Chrysis has persuaded my wife and daughter not

---

[1] I add explanations and comments between square brackets.

to admit a thing. She is clinging to the baby and refuses to let it go. So don't be surprised if I murder her.' 'Murder my woman?' 'Yes, she knows all about it.' 'No, Nikeratos, you must not.' 'But I wanted to tell you first.' 'The man's mad,' concludes Demeas as Nikeratos rushes back in. [But he was in his own way logical. He wanted to cover up the affair by destroying the child. If that made it necessary to kill Chrysis he would at the same time eliminate a possible witness. Being slow-minded he had not as yet connected Moschion with his daughter.]

Demeas thinks it will be best to tell him the truth. But before he can move to do so, Chrysis rushes out with the baby, pursued by Nikeratos; when Demeas calls to her to run into his house, she cannot believe her ears. He has to repeat the order twice, while he grapples with Nikeratos and claims that the child is his. Thwarted, Nikeratos proposes to kill his own wife; Demeas stops him, and offers to tell him the facts. At long last this puts into his head the suspicion that his friend's son had been responsible for his daughter's misfortune. Demeas, wishing to shield his son from the other's resentment and to soften the blow to the other's pride, assures him that the boy, though innocent, will marry her; she must have been, like Danaë, the victim of a god. Nikeratos is not convinced but does not know how to argue against this theory; accepting necessity, he goes in to complete the preparations for the wedding.

Once again nothing seems to stand in the way of the marriage.

Act V. But now Moschion returns home and declares that although he had at first felt nothing but relief at being cleared of suspicion, on thinking things over he had become so angry with his father that he had quite lost control of himself. If it were not that he was so attached to the girl, he would not give him another chance of a similar misjudgment, but go off to the wars. That he cannot do, but he will pretend to do it, to give his father a fright and teach him to behave better in future. Taking himself very seriously, he speaks in an elaborate style approaching that of tragedy. He stops at the entrance of Parmenon, who also reflects. He had been foolish to run away; he had done nothing wrong; he had nothing to do with the birth of the child; Moschion it was who had brought it to the house; one of the household had claimed to be its mother. 'He threatened to brand me. There you've got it. There's not a straw to choose between suffering that justly or unjustly; it's not a nice thing, however it is done.'

Moschion interrupts his ruminations with an order to fetch him out a sword and a military cloak, and as the puzzled slave goes in forecasts that his father will beg him to stay, and that he will refuse for a time but at length give in. But Parmenon returns without having fulfilled his task. He has found that they are both behind the times; the wedding-feast is going forward and it is time to fetch the bride. Moschion loses his temper, hits him in the face and drives him back; then the horrid thought strikes him that his father may not play the part assigned, but angrily let him go.

But there is no opportunity for reconsideration. Parmenon returns with the sword and cloak, and reports that not a soul had noticed him on his errand; so let Moschion get on his way. The stratagem has miscarried; play-acting has not attracted the desired audience. Yet no sooner has the expectation of the father's appearance been dashed, than he does come out, with a different motive, namely to look for the missing bridegroom. 'What's the idea of dressing like that?' he exclaims on seeing him, and then takes neither of the courses that Moschion had envisaged.

He says that he likes him for being angry, but that he should remember all that had been done for him from childhood. 'I accused you unjustly. I was under a misapprehension, I made mistakes, I was mad. But while I treated others wrongly, you see how I cared for your interests; I remained silent about those false suspicions, one and all, I kept them to myself, and did not exhibit them for our enemies' glee. But you are now making my mistake public and calling others to witness my folly. It's not what I expect, Moschion. Don't remember the one day of my life when I was utterly wrong and forget all the days that went before. I could say more but will not.'

Moschion is too young to match the candour of this sympathetic reproof. He is saved from making a reply by the appearance of Nikeratos, escaping from the fuss made by his wife over the preparations for the wedding. Seeing Moschion apparently prepared to leave home, he proposes to arrest him for the rape of his daughter. The boy with vain attempts to maintain his dignity welcomes this as a way of escape from his false position, but Demeas intervenes, telling Nikeratos to bring out the bride at once. Reassured, he does so and the happy ending, so long desired and so often postponed, is reached at last.

That is the plot of *Samia*. Let us now consider some of its features. First, although the play is called after her, and although she is an essential and often prominent piece in its structure, she makes only three brief appearances on the stage. This gives little opportunity for drawing her character, yet she is designed to arouse keen sympathy. In the first scene her readiness to help the young pair and her concern for the baby's welfare are made more prominent than her willingness to father a child on Demeas, and it is not pointed out that she will so further her own interests. The insults with which Demeas expels her, ignorant as she is of their cause, win her our support. Later, threatened by Nikeratos, she shows loyal courage in sticking to the story concocted with Moschion and the other women.

With the fifth act she fades into the background; Moschion's marriage, preparations for which have been a constantly recurring theme throughout the play, becomes an increasingly important motive. The play had an alternative title, *Kedeia*, or *Connection by Marriage*, and this has the justification that one theme is the manner in which this marriage, universally desired, is frustrated over and over again by the emotions of those closely concerned.

Alternate acts open with monologues addressed to the audience, by Moschion in Acts I and V, by Demeas in Act III. That in Act V is considerably shorter than that in Act I, in accord with the increasing pace of the play as it progresses. Like Moschion, Demeas has two monologues, but in the same act, and for him too the second is the shorter. Acts II and IV are mainly dialogue, but begin with short monologues by two persons who enter one after the other and are not immediately aware of one another's presence; in Act IV the scheme is extended by the entry of a third person who gives his short monologue while the other two converse apart.

In the second half of the play the rapid succession of events and situations, which often cheats expectation, is noteworthy. Menander's writing is often very economical and requires of the spectator a quick and sympathetic recognition of what is afoot. More modern dramatists often proceed in a more leisurely way. Consider for example these exchanges from the opening of a scene in Goldsmith's *She Stoops to Conquer*:

> *Mrs Hardcastle.* Confusion! thieves! robbers! we are cheated, plundered, broke open, undone.
> *Tony.* What's the matter, what's the matter, mamma? I hope nothing has happened to any of the good family!
> *Mrs Hardcastle.* We are robbed. My bureau has been broken open, the jewels taken out, and I'm undone.

In Menander that *might* have run:

> *Mrs Hardcastle.* Thieves! We are plundered, broke open.
> *Tony.* What's the matter, mamma? I hope none of the family——
> *Mrs Hardcastle.* The jewels are taken and I'm undone.

Yet Menander varies his pace and sometimes disguises his speed by otiose oaths and parenthetical phrases, 'by the gods' and 'tell me now'. He can make a woman enter with the line

Oh what a misfortune! what a misfortune! what a misfortune!

Samia offers no profound study of character. But each individual is lifelike. For the most part he does not explain himself, but one can guess the emotions and considerations which lie behind his words and his actions. This is the way one reacts to people in real life, if one has any interest in them. To do it requires some imagination, but the spoken word is more revealing than the written, and no doubt the actor interpreted and reinforced his text.

Demeas is a man who tries to act calmly, but it is an effort for him to do so, and the forcible repression of his temper makes its explosion more powerful when it comes. Towards his social equals, that is those of citizen status, he is considerate; he amuses himself, to be sure, by playing with the ingenuous Nikeratos, but again and again he treats him tactfully, being aware of his irascibility. But the slave Parmenon is for him an inferior being for whom he has no respect; he is to be handled with the threat of a whipping and with a lie. Moschion shares his father's attitude; made impatient by the slave's well-meaning attempt to convey a piece of good news, he cuts his lip with a blow.

It is not clear that the play has any moral or is anything but a very successful entertainment. It might be regarded as a warning against deceit. The passing-off of the child is the cause of all the trouble that assails Demeas, Chrysis, Moschion and even Nikeratos. The pretence of going off to the wars lands Moschion in an awkward place. But if it was intended as such a warning, the effect is weakened by the fact that without the deceit the young people's baby would have doubtless been exposed in order to conceal the illegitimate birth. Thus the final result is better than it would have been if all had honourably refused to father the child on Demeas. Even Moschion's pretence leads to a useful clearing of the air between him and his father.

Similar observations can be made about other plays. *Perikeiromene* may discourage outrages caused by jealousy; but without that perpetrated on Glykera she would not have found her father or achieved marriage with Polemon. *Epitrepontes* may suggest that a man should be as loyal to his wife as she to him; but if Charisios had taken that advanced view from the beginning, he would never have recovered his child.

Menander's plays always involve at least one well-to-do household, and the obtaining of a wife or lover by one of its members. Money is important, intellectual pursuits, literature, art or philosophy are not. Hence he is sometimes accused of being confined to the interests and morality of a bourgeois society.

Some critics have gone further with such judgments as that he depicts an imaginary society, 'a world outside time and space, which knows only seduced girls and frivolous youths, crafty slaves, depraved procurers, stupid fathers and so on, a world in which there is only love and money.' The untruth of these words, which were indefensible even when they were

written, has been underlined by every discovery of new
Menandrean texts. It would be as true, and as false, to say
that his world knows only innocent girls and hard-working
young men, loyal slaves and understanding fathers. There
are, it must be admitted, no high-minded procurers. Menander's world is a real world, in that it contains a whole
spectrum of characters ranging from good to bad, and there
are few of the bad without some redeeming feature and few of
the good without some human fault. Nor is it true that it
contains nothing but love and money. It contains friendship,
loyalty, jealousy, determination, pique, malice, respect, all
the web of emotions that colour human relations.

What is true is that Menander's is a selective world in the
sense that if we take all his surviving work as constituting a
'world', it is one in which certain events, notably rape, kid-
napping, and the recovery of long-lost children, and perhaps
certain characters, like hetairai, soldiers and slave-traders,
occurred more frequently than they did in the life of contemporary Athenians. A single play may associate a number
of these over-represented factors and their association will be
statistically improbable. But it is not impossible; these were
all things that happened and persons who could exist and meet
in reality. A dramatist is not a statistician.

Aristophanes had claimed that he would 'teach' or 'advise'
his hearers; there was a long tradition in Greece that the poet
was an educator. Was it still living in Menander's day? Could
he have claimed, in Horace's words, to mix what was useful
with what was pleasant? A speaker in Plutarch's *Table-Talk*
(712 B) thinks that he could have done, praising his 'good
simple maxims, which slip in to soften even the most rigid
character and bend it to a better shape'. Such maxims, often
single lines, were collected by anthologists for the sake of their
sentiments, and may have exerted an influence on those who
heard them spoken on the stage. Yet, as Plutarch's speaker
noticed, in their context they do not call attention to themselves but arise naturally; indeed even a close search brings to
light fewer than might have been expected. Sometimes they

are not without a touch of irony, as the man who utters the sentiment does so with comical earnestness or inappropriately or maliciously.

The phrase:

> Whom the gods love, die young

could be interpreted as resigned pessimism or beautiful consolation, if we did not know that it was in fact spoken to infuriate an old man. The line:

I am a man; and think nothing that is human to be not mine

often sentimentally praised for its nobility, was spoken by an inquisitive man, who proves to be unaware of his son's love-affair and unsympathetic when he learns of it.

More important is the general moral atmosphere of the plays. Crime does not pay; greed is ugly; kindness and understanding are primary virtues. The human being is a weak creature, liable to make mistakes, and the sport of chance; yet there is nothing finer than a man, that is one who lives up to what a man should be, who knows his limits and his possibilities, who is generous to forgive and to help his friends. The virtues that belong to private life are required of everybody, and the plays give their approval to those who practise them and withhold it from those who fall short, reserving ridicule for the avaricious, the pompous, the insincere, and for fathers who have forgotten what it is like to be young.

6

Drama at Rome

ALTHOUGH the Romans eventually dominated Italy, they began as one of many peoples, some of whom were culturally more advanced than they. They took the opportunity to become great borrowers, in art, in religion and in literature. More often than not they were able to give a new turn and a Roman character to what they borrowed.

Around the coasts of Sicily and southern Italy Greeks had settled from the eighth century onwards and their cities, although politically independent, shared the civilisation of the old country. The most important communities were Syracuse, where one can still sit in their great theatre, and Taras, or Tarentum as the Romans called it (modern Taranto), the chief city in Apulia. Nearest to Rome was Naples (Neapolis), from which Greek influence spread northwards and no doubt reached Rome, whose protection the Neapolitans had accepted by the beginning of the third century BC. The Tarantines were more obstinate and were conquered, perhaps as early as 272; the Syracusans entered into treaties with Rome but, having deserted her during the Second Punic War, were subjected in 212.

Even nearer to Rome were the Etruscans, generally thought to have been invaders from Asia Minor, who formed the ruling classes in Etruria, the territory on the other side of the Tiber. Their language remains a mystery, although they wrote in Greek characters. They became great customers for the finest Greek pottery and grew familiar with Greek mythology, which was illustrated not only on that but also on metal work; local craftsmen then imitated these models.

Although the Etruscans were finally conquered and their culture was extinguished, for a long time it exercised a powerful influence on Rome. A passage in Livy (7.2), although it may be suspected of having a large element of guess-work, seems to preserve a memory of an Etruscan origin for early performances intended to entertain the crowd. There was at Rome an old annual festival, the *Ludi Romani*,[1] held in September to reverence Jupiter; a procession was held in his honour, followed by a chariot-race and exhibitions of equestrian skill. In 363 B C, according to Livy, in the hope of mollifying the gods, who had inflicted a pestilence upon the city,

> players were introduced from Etruria who, dancing to the music of a piper, but not singing themselves or miming any representation of song, moved not ungracefully in the Etruscan manner. Young men began to imitate them, bandying jokes in rough verses, and their movements did not discord with their voices. Native Roman professional performers were given the name of *histriones* because a player was in Etruscan called *ister*; they did not follow the earlier practice (? of the young amateurs) which alternated irregular unpolished improvised lines similar to the Fescennine verses,[2] but presented medleys rich in music, with song fitted to the strains of the pipe and suitable movements to go with it.

All these entertainments are thought of as preceding true drama. Some support for the belief that they had an origin in Etruria is given by the probability that the Latin words for stage, *scaina*, and mask, *persona*, are Etruscan deformations of the Greek *skene* and *prosopon*.

Livy's references to the improvised jesting of the young amateurs look like an attempt to provide a Roman ancestry for the so-called Atellan plays. Named after the town Atella in Campania, they are proved by allusions in Plautus to have been familiar at Rome at the end of the third century; they may have been imported much earlier. Originally they were in Oscan, an Italic language but one which cannot have been intelligible to many in Rome; on being adopted there they must have changed their language to Latin, or at least modified

---

[1] *Ludi*, traditionally and inadequately translated as 'Games', were public holidays with a kernel of religious ceremonial. But as 'holy days' developed into 'holidays', the amusement of the crowds became of increasing importance.

[2] These may have had their name from the Etruscan town of Fescennium; their nature is obscure.

their dialect. Like the Commedia dell' Arte they had a nucleus of stock characters; all of them wore grotesque masks and were marked by greed, gluttony and folly. Some names are known: Maccus, Bucco, Pappus, Manducus, Dossennus. At first the dialogue seems to have been largely impromptu; a situation will have been invented, which the amateur actors developed with rough jokes and raillery. It was only in the early first century that Pomponius and Novius wrote texts for the Atellan performers, apparently short pieces which were used to close the proceedings after a day given over to tragedies; typical titles are *Maccus the Innkeeper, Maccus the Soldier, Maccus in Exile, Bucco Adopted, Pappus' Bride, A Nanny-goat, The Fullers.* The surviving fragments from these plays rarely exceed a single line, are often coarse, and contain much unusual vocabulary, for the sake of which they have been preserved; alliteration is insistently noticeable.

Another kind of local drama seems to be represented on many vases painted in southern Italy, particularly Apulia, for the most part during the fourth century B C. Many of them show a low stage, often with access in the centre by steps, five to seven in number; when no steps are drawn, the artist may just have omitted them to simplify his picture. The stage is usually supported by plain square timber props, but occasionally stands on round pillars with capitals. The space below it is sometimes concealed by draperies. The stage does not appear to be a wide one, but that may be due to the limitations imposed by painting on a vase; sometimes it is protected by an overhanging roof. On several vases the wooden wall behind it has first floor windows, from which women look out; characters may bring ladders to reach them. Sometimes there is a highly decorated door, placed at the side, perhaps for artistic convenience, to leave the centre free for figures; masks, garlands, bowls and jugs seem to hang on the wall. It is possible, however, that the artist did not intend a realistic picture, but simply filled empty spaces with objects used in the play. A similar problem attends the small trees which he sometimes draws; he may merely have wished to indicate an outdoor scene, or there may have been saplings or branches thrust between the planks of the stage. But altars, chairs and tables will have been real stage properties.

The actors wear tights, usually ill-fitting, often a huge phallus, padding and an extremely grotesque mask. That they are servants of Dionysus seems to be shown by several vases which depict him on the stage with them. The scenes in which they appear are partly travesties of mythology and partly taken from contemporary life. An old man tries to drag a woman away from a young man, who has however the better hold on her; a slave steals food; slaves are tied up and beaten. Heracles is a favourite figure in the mythological scenes, portrayed as a glutton or as a bully, threatening Apollo or even Zeus. An amusing fragment shows Ajax, traditionally the ravisher of Cassandra, clasping the statue of Athena in a terrified plea for sanctuary, as Cassandra drives her knee into his back and pulls off his helmet; a priestess recoils in horror.

Although these vases may have been inspired by Athenian plays imported into the West during the period of Middle Comedy, the actors are more generally supposed, with some plausibility, to be the *phlyakes* of southern Italy, who had some similarity to the *deikeliktai* of Sparta (see p. 53), and who were given literary standing by Rhinthon of Tarentum about 300 B C. He wrote plays in verse for them, which were called *hilaro-tragoidiai*, 'merry tragedies'.

Unfortunately there is nothing to show that the *phlyakes* had any influence on the development of drama at Rome. It is true that Livius Andronicus, who is credited by Livy with the decisive step of introducing plot into stage performances, perhaps was by origin a captive Greek from Tarentum, but his ambition seems to have been to introduce the Romans to good Greek literature. He translated the *Odyssey* into the old-established local metre of 'Saturnians', and when in 240 he exhibited a tragedy and a comedy at the *Ludi Romani*, the scanty evidence suggests that his models were classical Greek tragedy and New Comedy; certainly he used Greek metres for both kinds of drama.

His example was quickly followed by a native Italian, Gnaeus Naevius, from Campania; active from 235 to 204 or 201, he wrote an original epic on the First Punic War, a few tragedies on Greek subjects and one or two historical plays on themes from Roman history, but his dramatic work was mostly in comedy. The titles survive of more than thirty such plays; nearly half are Greek words, often known to have been used as titles of Greek New Comedy. It is probable then that he usually translated Greek dramas, but possible that he also tried his hand at composing new comedies with a setting in Italy: *Ariolus*, or *The Soothsayer*, a fragment from which speaks of hosts at (or guests from) Praeneste and Lanuvium, towns near Rome, may have been one such (see p. 115).

It is not surprising that when the Romans began to develop a literature of their own, they should have been dependent on the highly advanced productions of the Greeks. What is not altogether clear is how knowledge of these works reached them and how they obtained them. Probably there were visitors and immigrants from the Greek cities of southern Italy, some of whom may even have originated in mainland Greece; they may have brought books with them. That not a few educated Romans could read Greek even as early as the late third century is suggested by the fact that Fabius Pictor, the first Roman historian, wrote in Greek, setting a fashion which lasted for a couple of generations.

However that may be, there was a ready audience for the plays of these early authors, which, being adapted from Greek models, dealt with Greek mythology, if they were tragedies, and represented Greek characters, if they were comedies. From 214 four days were devoted to stage-performances at the *Ludi Romani*. The 'Plebeian Holiday', instituted in 220 and held in November, the first of several festivals intended to keep up civilian morale in the Second Punic War, may have had a day of drama from the first, although the earliest recorded performance is that of Plautus' *Stichus* in 200. The 'Holiday of the Great Mother', a goddess brought from Phrygia in Asia Minor, was instituted in 204 and held in April; drama was probably a feature from the beginning. There is no evidence for the giving of plays at the 'Holiday of Apollo', begun in 212 with a date in July, at any time before 169, but this may be no more than an accident. Besides these regular festivals there were occasional opportunities for dramatic productions, perhaps at the 'Great Holidays', irregularly held for specific purposes, and certainly at some 'funeral games' in honour of eminent men. This growth of interest no doubt encouraged the ambitions of the most original of all writers for the Roman theatre, known to later Romans by the name of Plautus, whose earliest plays belong to the last decade of the third century.

Many of the stages shown on the vases from Apulia (p. 115) look like temporary structures. It is certain that the plays of Naevius and Plautus were presented on a temporary wooden stage in front of a temporary wooden building with three doors; in this the actors assembled and dressed. Facing this there was seating, perhaps benches; but there is no evidence to indicate how extensive it was; probably some spectators had to stand at the back. From early in the second century the front rows were reserved for senators.

There was no permanent theatre at Rome before 55 BC, when one was built by Pompey (see Fig. 2); it was associated with a temple for Venus and colonnades where spectators could take refuge from a storm; there seem to have been seats for about 10,000 in the auditorium. An attempt had been made in 155 to erect a stone theatre, but it had foundered on the opposition of those who thought play-acting immoral. But in the first century the temporary theatres had become elaborate; linen awnings protected the spectators from the sun; there must have been rising tiers of scaffolded seating and the stage-building was lavishly decorated. The theatre built by the aedile Aemilius Scaurus in 58 became notorious for its extravagance; the elder Pliny's account, written some 125 years later, may be exaggerated, but even so is revealing. He alleges that it could seat 80,000 spectators, that it had a stage-building of three storeys, the lowest of marble, the middle one of glass, and the top one of gilded planks; standing between the 360 columns that decorated it were 300 bronze statues.

Clearly this stage-building was architecturally like those of later permanent theatres of which the best known is that of Orange in southern France. They had a semicircular *orchestra* in front of a stage longer than the diameter of the semicircle, which was used not for dancing, but for reserved seats; at Rome they were kept for senators and their families. Behind the stage rose a building decorated with tiers of columns and having doors in its lowest storey. It was as wide and often as high as the auditorium, to which it was joined at each end by a tall structure which spanned the entrances to the orchestra.

Thus the spectators sat in a space which was, in contrast to that of a Greek theatre, enclosed; even the sky above was excluded by the awnings; a small theatre could actually be roofed, like that at Pompeii, constructed about 80 BC. It may be guessed that this design was established at Rome before the year 68 BC, when the legislation of Otho gave the *equites* (men with a property qualification of 400,000 sesterces) the right to occupy the front fourteen rows behind the *orchestra*.

The audience of the first century was representative of all social classes, and the same seems to have been true in Plautus' days. Admission was free, expenses being borne by the aediles in charge of the festival, who disposed of some state funds but often supplemented them from their own pockets. They hoped that this liberality would have its reward when they presented themselves to the electors as candidates for higher office. In choosing to present plays adapted from the refined work of Greek dramatists they must have been trying to attract the favour of the more intelligent members of the population, for whom serious drama was a comparatively new experience. Others however were free to come and had to be reckoned with. The prologue to Plautus' *Poenulus* or *Little Carthaginian*, whether designed for its first performance or for a revival, shows what could happen. The attendants are asked not to walk in front of the spectators' faces nor to show anyone to a seat while an actor is on the stage, since latecomers ought to stand; slaves are not to grab seats, but leave room for the free men; it is in fact suggested that they will, if discovered, be driven out by blows from the rod-carrying officials. Nursemaids should look after their infant charges at home and not bring them to see the show, where they will cause annoyance by bleating like little goats. Married women are to watch silently and laugh silently, check the tinkle of their voices, and keep their chatter for their homes.

Not only was the audience one with less knowledge and appreciation of drama than was usual among the Greeks, it was also one with less respect for those who performed it. In Greece all in the cast were servants of Dionysus, and the leading actor in each play had his name preserved in the official records. At Rome, by the time of Cicero at least, most actors were slaves with Greek names, and this continued to be the rule in the first century A.D. They will have belonged to a free man, who may himself have appeared on the stage with them. This arrangement was perhaps already the custom at the end of the third century. The prologue to Plautus' *Asinaria*, speaking of the company and its master, uses words commonly applied to slaves and their owner, and jokes, if jokes they are, like that at the end of his *Cistellaria*—'they'll remove their costumes and any actor who has made a mistake will get a beating'—point the same way.

But free men played along with the slaves. Titus Publilius Pellio took the leading parts in Plautus' *Stichus* and *Epidicus* and Lucius Ambivius Turpio was well known in Terence's days. Actors were, however, regarded as somewhat disreputable; they were not allowed to serve in the army, were deprived of a vote,[1] and were subject to the *coercitio* of the magistrates, that is to say could be beaten, imprisoned, or exiled at will. Although the emperor Augustus restricted this power to the days of the festival, he used it to inflict a public flogging on a man who had caused a married Roman woman to cut her hair and take the role of a boy, perhaps in a mime (see p. 116). It is true that a few actors obtained a footing in society; the most famous was Publius Roscius Gallus, who won the favour of Sulla, receiving from him admission to the order of the *equites*, and who was defended by Cicero in a court case of 67 or 66 B C concerning a slave-actor of whom Roscius was part-owner. et Yin some quarters Sulla's association with a man of his profession was regarded as an enormity.

One might suppose that slaves with Greek names spoke Latin with a foreign accent. If this was so, it need not have been an unqualified handicap. The plays which were of greatest importance in the time of the Roman Republic, that is down to the middle of the first century B C, were adaptations of Greek and their characters were Greeks. It would then not have seemed altogether unnatural if they spoke their Latin like Greeks. Another relevant point is that actors did not attempt to give a close illusion of natural, ordinary speech as they declaimed their parts, which were written in verse, and large parts of which were delivered to a musical accompaniment. 'They do not utter their words,' writes Quintilian (*Inst. Or.*

[1] These disabilities did not apply to actors in Atellan plays.

2.10.13), 'quite in the manner in which we ordinarily speak, which would lack art, nor do they depart far from nature, a fault which would destroy mimicry.'

Among the Greeks, as has been seen (p. 78, plays of the New Comedy were sometimes, and perhaps normally, performed by three actors, who doubled the parts, assisted by mute supers. At Rome there was not such a strict limitation; there are many plays which require at least five speaking actors. It is not known how many were actually used since, although some doubling of parts is *a priori* likely, there is nothing to show its extent. All that is certain is that the speaker of the prologue might change his costume to appear as a character in the play proper.

Modern experience shows that it is possible for an audience to accept that a small change of costume, without any change in make-up, suffices to convert an actor from one role to another. Yet there is no doubt that in the Greek theatre the conversion was aided by the change of mask; the mask indicated what character was being played. Was doubling of parts similarly facilitated at Rome? Unfortunately it is disputed whether masks were worn in the Roman adaptations of Greek plays and the question, vital to the visualisation of the Roman theatre, admits of no confident answer.

There is no reason to doubt that the actors who performed Greek plays in Greek in the theatres of southern Italy and Sicily were masked. It would be natural to suppose that masks were worn in the Roman adaptations also, especially as this was the custom in the native Atellan drama. But Diomedes, a teacher of literature in the fourth century AD, reports that masks were introduced by Roscius to hide his squint; previously wigs had been worn. This may be derived from Varro, Roscius' scholarly contemporary, and it has been supported by an appeal to a passage of Cicero's dialogue *On the Orator* (3.221), where Crassus is made to say 'Everything depends on the face; there is the seat of all the mastery exerted by the eyes; and so those seniors of ours did better than us when they gave even Roscius no high praise when he wore a mask'. But an equally possible translation is 'because he wore a mask'; it is not necessary to suppose from this passage that he ever acted without one.

On the other hand the commentary derived from Donatus, which goes under his name and is contemporary with Diomedes, speaks of actors as 'still' being masked in the time of Terence. The contrast is with the conditions of the fourth century A.D. when masks had been abandoned and, it may be added, actresses played the female parts. Those who support the story about Roscius think that Donatus ignorantly believed masks had been used from the first.

Attempts to determine the credibility of Diomedes are inconclusive. References in the plays to change of facial expression are irrelevant; similar phrases are found in Greek plays; the audience can use its imagination. Roscius' alleged reason for adopting the mask (and making his company follow suit) seems frivolous and does not explain why other companies, who presumably did not squint, also took to wearing masks. It can only be thought that they found the practice in some way advantageous. But if it was advantageous, it is strange that it was not taken over from the Greeks originally.

In Plautus' *Amphitruo* Mercury and Jupiter take on the likenesses of Sosia and Amphitruo, and in order that the audience may distinguish them from the men they impersonate Mercury wears wings in his hat and Jupiter a golden lock of hair, signs which, it is explained, are invisible to the other characters. It can be argued with some plausibility that if no masks were worn these distinguishing marks would be unnecessary; yet perhaps they would be welcomed by the less keen-sighted or more distant spectators in a large theatre. Again, although masks would be even more convenient in this play, since no company would include two pairs of identical twins, than they would be in *Menaechmi*, Shakespeare's play *The Comedy of Errors* shows that they are not necessary.

None of the above considerations, nor others of even less force, suffice to settle the question. Many scholars have no hesitation in accepting the evidence of Diomedes. My own inclination is to disbelieve him; but if he got his story from Varro—and this is no more than an inference from the fact that he several times quotes Varro as an authority for other matters—one could not refuse him credence.

Fortunately there is no doubt about a change that really was made from Greek practice of the early third century.

ΦΙΛΟΤΙΜΙΔΗΣ   ΧΑΡΙΣ   ΞΑΝΘΙΑΣ

3. Play scene. The actors, probably phylakes, wear tights; the slave has filched some of the delicious food. *From a Greek vase made in Southern Italy c. 370 B.C.*

4. Actor from the Roman stage, probably representing a slave.

Menander's plays were of five acts, separated by intermezzi provided by the chorus. The absence of a chorus from the Roman theatre meant that Plautus and Terence did not write in acts but for continuous performance. It is possible that their Greek contemporaries did the same; there is no evidence. In modern texts the plays of Plautus are divided into five acts, but these were first introduced in an edition of 1514 by Nicolà Angelio, who took up a proposal made by G. B. Pio in 1500. The division of Terence into acts dates from antiquity, although it puzzled scholars how to make him fit their scheme.

The disappearance of the five-act structure presented the Latin dramatists with problems. The plays they were adapting had used the intermezzi to mark the passage of time. How were they to mark it? More often than not they ignored the difficulty. This is perhaps not an adverse criticism. It is quite possible for an audience to understand that a momentarily empty stage represents a lapse of time. Shakespeare wrote for continuous performance and his audiences, modern or Elizabethan, accept or accepted this convention. But it is a convention easier to accept because successive scenes are normally to be thought of as occurring in different places; the spatial disruption facilitates the temporal disruption. Carried in imagination from one spot to another, the spectator can be easily carried also from one hour to another.

The action of the Greek play, however, took place in a single locality, usually outside the houses of two of the characters. If the text were translated into Latin without change, the audience would not know whether to think of an empty stage as empty for a time no longer than that during which the actors left it or whether it conventionally represented a longer period. Sometimes a phrase at the beginning of the scene that followed the break could indicate that time had passed. But the Latin authors seem often to have taken it for granted that this was not a thing over which spectators would bother their heads, or that they would have a clear sense of time.

This disregard is strikingly illustrated by Plautus' treatment in his *Bacchides* (*The Bacchis Sisters*) of the division between the first two acts of its original, *Dis Exapaton* (*A Double Deceit*). Plautus' play leaves no doubt that towards the end of the first act Menander's Moschos left for the market, and that shortly

113

afterwards the two girls whom he proposed to entertain prudently retreated indoors, having seen the approach of the rowdy chorus; its intermezzo covered the time of the shopping-expedition, from which Moschos returned at the beginning of the second act. In Plautus, Pistoclerus (his name for Moschos) leaves for the market at line 100, and is seen by the girls returning at 106; they mistake him for some unknown rowdy and retreat indoors, while he comes on the stage with his purchases at 110. It is true that Menander's plays require no strict correspondence of stage-time with that of events off-stage; five lines of a dialogue may cover happenings inside a house that would take at least five minutes to transact; but longer intervals, like those of a visit to the market or a journey to the country, are always covered by a choral interlude. There is never anything so offensive to a sense of time as this scene in Plautus.

But Plautus did on occasion take steps to overcome the difficulties caused by the absence of a chorus. His treatment of the division between Acts II and III of this same play is described below (p. 131). In *Curculio* he was faced with the problem that three characters left the stage at the end of the third act and entered again, some time having elapsed, at the beginning of the next. Their exit and immediate re-entry might have caused some bewilderment. The difficulty was solved by bringing on the man who provided costumes and properties, whether in person or represented by an actor. He says that one of the characters in the play, who has just left the stage, is such a scoundrel that he wonders whether he will get his properties back from him; after this joke, depending on identification of the character with the actor, he continues that while they wait for the man's return he will give the audience a kind of directory to Rome. In *Pseudolus* (537) the slave goes indoors to think out a plan of action, promising that he will soon be back and that meanwhile the audience will be entertained by the piper. The Greek original probably here had a division between acts and a choral interlude. Nothing suggests that such interludes were normally replaced at Rome by a piper's solo. This is a unique unrepeated experiment.

Such difficulties would of course not have arisen if the theatre had, like those of today, possessed a drop-curtain which could have been lowered to indicate the passage of time. But unsophisticated spectators might have supposed the play to have ended. A curtain that could separate the audience from the stage seems not to have been invented before the end of the second century BC. Even then it was stowed in a slot in the floor from which it was raised at the end of a play. Cicero says that this was a convenient method of concluding a mime (see p. 116), which as a formless kind of entertainment had no natural end. That the curtain was invented for that purpose is no more than a guess; at Rome it was richly embroidered and it may have been introduced to provide a spectacle before or between plays. The modern method, by which the curtain is raised to reveal the stage, appears to have been discovered before the latter part of the second century AD.

Some attempts were made, perhaps even before the middle of the second century BC, to write comedies not only in Latin but also about Italian life and characters. These were called *fabulae togatae*, 'plays dressed in togas', in distinction from *fabulae palliatae*, 'plays in Greek cloaks'. Of course not all characters wore an outer garment in either genre, but enough did so to make the distinction effective.

These plays would have been informative to the social historian; it is our misfortune that nothing survives except some titles, some brief quotations, and occasional references made by the authors of antiquity. Apparently the scene was never in Rome, but always in some small Italian town. For the most part the characters were, in contrast with those of Greek New Comedy, drawn from the lower ranks of society. Nevertheless it was unusual to portray a slave as being cleverer than his master; that might occur among the Greeks; things were better ordered in Italy. Women may have played a more active part than they did in most Greek comedies; this would reflect the difference between Greek and Italian social life.

Seneca (*ep.* 8.8.) says that *togatae* had an element of seriousness and were on a level somewhere between comedy and tragedy. The fragments quoted by grammarians for the sake of their colloquial language do not suggest any elevation of style. Perhaps he refers to a fondness for moral maxims. Lucius Afranius, more or less a contemporary of Terence's, was the best remembered of these authors; he admitted borrowing phrases from Menander, and he may have borrowed incidents also. His drama then was not of purely Italian inspiration, but drew on the traditions of Greek comedy.

Afranius' plays were still acted long after his death. The audience at Rome would often cheer a line in a play old or new, if it could be given some topical application, and actors might try to elicit such a response. Cicero alleges that in the year 57, when Clodius was sitting in the theatre, the whole company in unison directed against him a line from Afranius' *The Pretender*:

The course and end of your life of vice.

This chorusing of words intended for a single actor indicates that neither players nor spectators set great store by dramatic illusion. Afranius was still staged in the time of Nero, when actors in his play *Fire* were allowed to keep furniture they rescued from a burning house, perhaps realistically represented.

Another form of drama, which by the middle of the first century B C occupied an important place in the Roman theatre, was the mime. It had its origin in players or troops of players who earned their bread by presenting scenes from life or romance, spoken in prose; they included both men and women and acted in bare feet and without masks; there seems to have been a frequent element of impropriety in their productions. They became part of the officially sponsored entertainment at many festivals, and in Cicero's time had come to be used as tail-pieces (*exodia*) after tragedies, ousting the Atellan farces that had previously been used.

Their popularity led to successful attempts to raise their standard and give them literary form; authors began to write them scripts in the verse-metres familiar from comedy. A Roman knight, Decimus Laberius (106–43), won much favour with the crowd; he wrote in a highly alliterative manner, used the vocabulary and grammar of the lower classes, and generously met their appetite for obscenity. Julius Caesar, during his dictatorship, offered him a large sum if he would appear on the stage as an actor in one of his own mimes. Had he refused, he might have been held to admit the unsuitability of his writing for a man of his station; if he accepted, he could be accused of being ready to do anything for money. He chose to interpret the offer as an irresistible command—'what man could deny anything to a being to whom the gods had granted everything?'—but revenged his loss of dignity by two lines which he spoke in the mime:

> Then, Romans, we destroy our liberty

and

> Many must he fear, whom many fear.

Several of his works have names which had been used for comedies, e.g. *Aulularia, Gemelli, Piscator,* and they may have contained scenes suggested by such plays. *Aquae Calidae, Augur, Compitalia, Sorores, Virgo,* recall the same titles given to *fabulae togatae.* Some relation between these and the mime must be assumed, although nothing specific can be said about it.

Publilius, brought as a slave-boy from Syria, was freed and educated and then performed in his own mimes all over Italy; finally he defeated all comers at Rome in 46 BC. He was remarkable for the number of his well-turned sentiments, expressed in the Latin of educated men. This did not cause his works to be read, but they were pillaged for their nuggets of wisdom, which were formed into an anthology; this, enlarged by spurious material, had a wide circulation under the Empire. Learned men loved to quote his epigrams:

> O life, so long for the wretched, so short for the happy!

and

> Luxury lacks much, avarice everything

and

> The cure for injury is to forget.

The ancients expected their poets to be teachers. So when it took literary form, even this disreputable type of drama was made to serve the cause of moral improvement.

7

Plautus

PLAUTUS, the most original and vigorous writer of Roman comedy, came from Sarsina in Umbria, half-way between modern Florence and Rimini. It was an Italian town subjected to the Romans a dozen years before his birth. Whether Plautus was his real name or one humorously adopted for professional purposes,[1] and whether he had been an actor before he was a writer are questions which admit of fascinating discussion but no certain answer; fortunately they are of no importance to the historian of drama. Nothing shows that he acted in or produced his own plays, but he gives a strong impression that he understood the theatre for which he wrote. He would have an inexperienced audience, not very quick in the uptake, and so it was necessary to proceed more slowly than a Greek dramatist would, to say things twice, to introduce reminders about essential elements in the plot, and above all not to allow the spectators to become bored. They did not require complete coherence nor expect that characterisation should be consistent; these are merits demanded by a theatre-goer who can take a wide view; what was important for Plautus was the immediate effect.

All his twenty-one surviving plays are adaptations of Greek

[1] Plautus is a known family name, originally like so many a nickname referring to a physical peculiarity; it means 'flat-footed'. But *planipes*, which also means 'flat-footed', was a name for an actor in a mime, who wore no shoes. It is possible that the author adopted the name Plautus to suggest a connection with that simple form of drama. In one prologue he calls himself, or is called, Maccus and in another either Maccus or Maccius Titus. Here there is certainly some depreciatory joke. Maccus was a stock stupid character in Atellan plays, but Maccius is a name known from real life. Later generations believed the dramatist to have been named Titus Maccius Plautus; perhaps he was, but scepticism is not amiss.

comedies.[1] Three and probably a fourth are from Menander, two from Diphilus, two from Philemon, one apparently from Alexis, all authors of the great period of New Comedy. Of the other twelve one is from an otherwise unknown Demophilus, but all the rest have anonymous originals. There is nothing to show that any of them came from the Greek dramatists who were his contemporaries or belonged to the immediately preceding generation. On the contrary some of their original authors certainly lived about a hundred years earlier than he, and may even have been members of the great trio of that time.

Unfortunately it is impossible to say how Plautus got hold of these Greek plays. They may have formed part of the repertory of the Artists of Dionysus, but it is no more than a plausible guess that these visited the theatres of Greek cities in southern Italy, and there is no evidence that Plautus had any contact with them or with southern Italy at all. Perhaps the players for whom he wrote in some way obtained texts with which they provided him. It would be rash to suppose that he always admired the plays he adapted or thought them particularly suitable for his purposes; he may have had to use what he could get.

However that may be, the Greek authors provided him with stories of ingenious construction and scenes of dramatic tension. When these were embroidered and diversified, when their jests were multiplied and their comic possibilities exploited by a writer who possessed an unfailing vigour of expression and a rich abundance of language there resulted a new kind of popular drama which could entertain a wide range of tastes.

Variety is the obvious device to hold the attention of any audience. Metrical variety had become less and less used by the Greeks, and it is possible that in Menander's later plays it was entirely abandoned, in order to maintain a homogeneous medium; but the choral intermezzi were still there, to provide a change of metre and the charms of music. Deprived of a chorus, Plautus re-introduced these elements into the body of his plays. Whether the first to do it or not, he increased the

---

[1] The twenty-first, *Vidularia*, survives only in the sense that a single manuscript preserves about one hundred lines, many mutilated.

number of scenes written in the long trochaic or iambic lines, and on the Roman stage, whatever may have been done in Greece, these were delivered to an accompaniment by the piper. This makes likely a manner of speech not quite like that adopted by the actors for the unaccompanied iambic senarii (lines of six feet). Certainly differences can be detected in the language employed; often the vocabulary has a more elevated tone, the sentences use a greater wealth of words, and opportunities are seized for sound-effects; in particular the Roman delight in alliteration was catered for.

But this was not Plautus' only metrical means to variety. Far more striking and far more individual to him were scenes in various other metres, mainly cretics, bacchiacs and anapaests, which had in Greece been associated with song. They became more and more common as time went on, and in the late *Casina*, if the prologue is excluded from the count, nearer a half than a third of the play proper is of this kind. Sometimes several metres are used in conjunction; there may even be change from line to line, as occurs in the lyrics of Greek tragedy.

It is customary today to call these scenes *cantica*. The word was used by Cicero, but the late grammarians' attempts to define its meaning are confused and unhelpful. There is no certainty that it had the same denotation for him as for us; it may have covered everything apart from the iambic senarii. It is derived from the verb *canere*, which we translate 'sing', but there are many different ways of interpreting the word 'sing'; we even talk of a 'sing-song' voice. Perhaps the minimum sense of *canere* is 'to speak with attention to pitch and rhythm'. It is possible that there was no fundamental difference in delivery between the long iambic and trochaic lines and what we call *cantica*.

Certainly the latter were not sung in the style of arias in grand opera; the words were important and often indeed essential to the progress of the play; the vocalist must have concentrated more on getting the meaning across than on the musical qualities of his 'song'. There are even lines which an accumulation of consonants make it almost impossible to sing, in the usual modern sense of the word. Here at least emphasis must have been more on rhythm than on notes. Nevertheless

there are passages in ancient authors which suggest that these
'lyrics' made greater demands on the voice, and it may be
that, particularly in the monologues, which are numerous,
the actor was required to produce sounds that we should
unhestitatingly call song.

Here may be mentioned an odd story in Livy; he says that
Livius Andronicus, who acted in his own plays, found his
voice giving way as a result of repeated encores and therefore
obtained leave to employ a slave to sing the words while he
put his unhampered energy into silent miming. This, Livy
asserts, was the origin of the custom by which someone sang
in time with the actors' gestures, the latter's voice being
required for the spoken scenes only.[1] Even if he had no opportunities himself to see literary dramas performed, he must
have known men old enough to have seen them. Yet if he
believed it to have been the normal custom for one person to
sing while another mimed, he must have been mistaken, since
Cicero speaks of the singing of the famous actor Roscius.

There has been much argument about possible precedents
for Plautus' use of *cantica*. At first sight an origin may be sought
in imitation of the sung lyrics, mostly monodies, which
became increasingly common in the tragedies of Euripides.
Plautus often used the form for passages of elevated tone,
whether meant to be pathetic or ridiculous, in which a
character laments his or her situation, and the language is
often singularly like that of serious laments to be found in the
fragments of Ennius, the leading tragedian of the early second
century. Both writers use much alliteration and assonance.
But Plautus was the older of the two; chronology forbids any
assumption that the initiative came from Ennius.

But whatever the origin of the *cantica*, they lend a peculiar
flavour to Plautus' plays. They could be enjoyed not only by
the mass of the audience, whom we can imagine to have been
readier to listen to a 'musical' than to a straight play, but also
by the more cultured hearer, who could appreciate the way in

[1] The first part of the story is credible. In London in November
1935 Mr Lupino Lane, having lost his voice, employed another
person to speak his part while he himself acted it. The device
caused such amusement that it was continued after Mr Lane's
recovery.

which changes of rhythm coincided with changes of feeling or subject.

By variety of metre and the use of musical numbers Plautus introduced into his Latin versions of plays that had belonged to Greek New Comedy elements that had formed part of the attraction of Old Comedy for its diversified audience. There were also other ways of responding to the simpler tastes of his spectators which recall features to be seen in Aristophanes. Nothing shows that he knew that writer's work, but he may have come across isolated precedents in the authors of New Comedy; on the other hand he may have acted independently, knowing what would please in the theatre; certainly, if he found any hints in his originals, he developed them vastly.

First, there is the spicing of scenes with indecencies, mostly sexual, often homosexual, and largely depending on ambiguous words. These passages seem to occur more at random than they do in Aristophanes; they may be completely absent from long stretches of text. Some few of them suit their speakers, but for the most part they stand out as inappropriate interruptions to the course of events; the actor momentarily becomes an entertainer with a line of dirty jokes.

Another kind of entertainment was provided by playing upon words, a device even more prominent in Plautus than in Old Comedy. This can be done with wit; it can be suitable to the speaker; it can be pregnant with meaning. Nothing could be more effective than Hamlet's

A little more than kin and less than kind.

But whereas it is credible enough that an excluded lover should make a bitter play on words as he upbraids the *pessuli pessumi* (most wicked bolts) which keep him out, or that a parasite should repeat syllables as he gloats over his expected dinner, *quanta sumini apsumedo, quanta callo calamitas* (What consumption there'll be of cow's udder, what damage I'll do to the flesh!), yet often Plautus aims at nothing more than creating a sound-effect by capping one word with another that is similar. This is just a game irrelevant to plot or character. But there are also puns and sometimes the similarity of words is made the basis for repartee, as when one character says

PLAUTUS

nihil sentio, and the other replies *non enim es in senticeto; eo non sentis*. That might be represented by

> (A) I'm not aware of anything. (B) No, you're not in a warehouse; that's why you're not aware.

Jokes of this sort can be heard in popular entertainments today.

Words were a source of delight for Plautus. Not only did he use a rich vocabulary drawn from colloquial speech, but he loved to invent comical new compounds and derivatives. His inventiveness and fancy did not desert him in his treatment of personal proper names. Greek New Comedy, as we have seen, used many over and over again for different characters. Since Plautus' audiences were not familiar with the conventions that attached each name to a particular type of person, he adopted the natural practice, usual in the modern theatre, of providing each character with his own individual name. In all his twenty-one plays there are only three instances of duplication: two young slaves called Pinacium, or 'Little Picture', two young men called Charinus, and two old men called Callicles. These names may have been taken over from the Greek originals, a procedure he sometimes followed, as for example in *The Bacchis Sisters* the slave Lydus kept his name from Menander's *A Double Deceit*. But the other slave in that play became Chrysalus instead of Syros, while the young men Sostratos and Moschos exchanged those names for the less trite Mnesilochus and Pistoclerus. The former was common in real life, Pistoclerus is not recorded, although a quite possible compound. This illustrates Plautus' normal practice: many of his names are genuine; many may be his own inventions, but they are made on correct principles by analogy with forms he knew. Some of the latter kind are intended to have some point: Pistoclerus is a loyal (*pistos*) friend. A soldier, who is probably a parvenu, is called Therapontigonus, 'Son of a Servant', a theoretically possible but improbable and ridiculous name. A few are openly comic, although correct, formations: a parasite Artotrogus, 'Nibbleloaf', and a moneylender Misargyrides, 'Money Haterson'. A few others, Pyrgopolinices, 'Forte Grandstrife', and Polymachaeroplagides, 'Mickledagger McStrike', which improperly combine three

123

elements, have parallels in Aristophanes' Tisamenophainippos and Panourgipparchides and conceivably had precedents in New Comedy, but are probably the products of his own fertile invention, like the magnificent double-barrelled Bumbomachides Clutumistaridisarchides.

These names, which have more point for those who know Greek, are only a particular case of a problem presented by the occurrence in Plautus' text of fairly numerous words of Greek origin, which are sometimes given Latin terminations or even compounded with a Latin element, e.g. *thermopotasti*, 'you've had a hot drink'. Are these words which had been adopted in the popular language of Rome? Or were they introduced to mark the fact that the characters were Greeks? Would they be understood by the majority of the audience or only by a select few? One is tempted to compare modern plays in which a foreigner speaks a line or two in his own tongue, which only a part of the audience will understand, but then considerately uses English, even to his compatriots, with occasional lapses into supposed vernacular expletives like '*Donnerwetter*'. But there are only a few places where one of Plautus' characters utters a phrase in Greek with apparently no reason but that he is a Greek. On the other hand there are many passages where Greek words are used with the apparent expectation that they will be understood by many in the theatre. A spectator will not resent elements that are above his head, provided that they are not excessive and that his own tastes are adequately catered for. A dramatist does not have to write down to the lowest level in his audience. Many French words have today a meaning for Englishmen who could not follow a French sentence, and similarly English is invading French. It may be guessed that Greeks, both slaves and free men looking for employment or trade, were already common enough in Rome to have made a considerable contribution to vocabulary.

Consistently with this Plautus seems to have relied on an elementary knowledge of Greek mythology among many of his audience. That his references to it were automatically translated from the original Greek, without any care whether they would be understood, was a theory once propounded by scholars unable to imagine how a successful dramatist works. It is quite untenable because these references occur not only in passages which may have a Greek origin but also in some which clearly are of his own composition. One need not suppose that every spectator had heard, for example, of Argus, but it was sufficient if many had done; and for those whose memories were hazy Plautus added a reminder: 'If Argus were their watcher, *he who was all eyes, whom Juno once attached as warder to Io,* he would never succeed in watching them.' Familiarity with Greek mythology will have come not only through contact with Greeks in person but also through its representation on works of art, which must have been explained and at least partially understood. Greek art and mythology had long been accepted by the Etruscans, the Romans' neighbours on the other side of the Tiber, from whom they received much cultural influence.

Another appeal to popular taste was provided by scenes in which characters exchange insults or threats. This seems to have been a standard form of entertainment in Italy. Horace recounts in the fifth satire of his first book how his travelling party, which included Maecenas and Virgil, were amused one night by the personalities exchanged by two 'parasites', a freed man and an Oscan (perhaps one should think of the Oscan plays from Atella) and the emperor Marcus Aurelius remembers another supper at which the company was diverted by the backchat between country-folk. Roman taste was also met by passages in which slaves are threatened with horrific and sometimes impossibly exaggerated physical maltreatment. The slaves themselves also anticipate or remember these punishments, frequently using comic language to refer to them.

Common to all this Plautine material is the characteristic of being designed for an immediate effect, to raise a laugh, without any regard for the progress of the action or appropriateness to the situation or to the character of the speaker, except in so far as scurrilities and foolish jokes are delivered mainly by slaves and men of low social standing. A standard motif developed for its own sake is the 'running slave', who often comes on in haste to deliver some piece of news, pretending to push aside invisible persons who crowd the street. Once Plautus doubles the absurdity by making such a slave, who carries information it is essential his master should have without delay, withold it when he finds him until he has indulged in a long passage of backchat (*Mercator* 111–75).

As Plautus introduces jokes for their own sake, the actors lose connection with the character they are portraying; they cease to represent Greeks in Athens, and become entertainers on the Roman stage. 'Don't you know, woman, why the Greeks called Hecuba a bitch?' A slave, boasting of his success in cheating his master, which he represents by military metaphors such as were dear to Plautus, concludes 'I am not having a triumph; that has become such a common thing these days'; he is referring to the frequency of triumphs celebrated by Roman generals in the early second century, perhaps to the year 189, which saw no fewer than four (*Bacchides* 1072).

Unconcerned though Plautus is to maintain dramatic illusion and ready to forget the plot temporarily, he was by no means indifferent to the story, but carried it on clearly, making the progress of the intrigue plain. For its main lines he was indebted to the Greek original and, particularly in early plays, he took pains to see that the spectators followed it. Thus in *Poenulus* the trick to deceive the slave-dealer is explained three times (170–87, 547–65, 591–603). The interruptions to the plot by the miscellaneous jokes may even be seen as testimony to its importance. Close attention was necessary to follow Menander's dramas and his rivals probably wrote in the same manner. Plautus, with an audience on which such demands could not be made, caused the play to proceed by shorter steps than the integrated acts of his models. Then, after a passage of light relief, he would often return to the thread of the plot by repeating a phrase which had immediately preceded the insertion.

Important though the plot was, Plautus was sometimes ready to truncate it. To take an example, in Diphilus' *Klerumenoi* (*Drawers of Lots*) a girl of free birth had been exposed, rescued, and brought up in a household where both father and son fell in love with her. The father hoped to obtain her by marrying her to a complaisant slave; his wife, taking the part of the son, who had been sent abroad, wished the bridegroom to be another slave, who would be ready to make way for him on his return. All analogy shows that the girl's free birth would be established and she be united with the young

126

man in legal marriage. But, says the prologue to *Casina*,[1] Plautus' adaptation,

> The youth will not come back to town today in this comedy. Don't expect it. Plautus was against it; he broke down a bridge on the young man's route.

The Latin poet was satisfied to concentrate on the earlier parts of the play, the manoeuvres of the husband and the wife, and the substitution, if that can be assigned to Diphilus, of a man for the girl in the bed where the father expected to find her.

Another way in which he altered the proportions of his originals appears in those plays where, as has been securely established, he greatly expanded and elaborated the role of a slave, making him much more prominent than he had been in the Greek. Three of these have as their title the name of a slave whose part was probably taken by the leading actor, as that of Chrysalus must have been in *The Bacchis Sisters*.[2]

Plautine slaves are of two main types, the ingenious trickster and the loyal servant. The former not only carries out the intrigue invented by the Greek author but is given to boasting elaborately of his cleverness; the supreme example is Chrysalus, who in a long *canticum* compares himself to Ulysses and the other characters to various figures who had parts, on either side, in the Trojan War. These slaves are sometimes incredibly insolent to their masters, in a manner which Plautus found it amusing to ascribe to servants of Greeks, who had strange ideals about freedom of speech. The honest retainers, on the other hand, often moralise at length about duty to their masters, uttering sentiments that would be highly approved by the slave-owners in the audience. Plautus may have found hints in his originals for what he so developed, but the prominence he gave it was his own.

[1] The original title was *Sortientes*, a literal translation of Diphilus' title; *Casina* seems to be that of a revival.

[2] At one point Chrysalus says 'It's not the act but the hatefulness of the actor that cuts me to the quick; *Epidicus* is a play that I love as I love myself, but there is none I watch with more distaste when Pellio acts it.' For the moment he is no longer Chrysalus but the actor who is Pellio's rival.

In 1968 publication of a papyrus containing parts of a section of Menander's *Dis Exapaton* which correspond to *Bacchides* 494–562 threw new light on the subject of Plautus' independence; it was found that he had made quite unsuspected changes. To explain the situation it will suffice to say that Mnesilochus had, while abroad in Ephesus to collect some money belonging to his father, fallen in love with a hetaira who was about to be taken to Athens. He wrote to his friend Pistoclerus there, asking him to find the girl, with whom he hoped to resume relations on his return. Pistoclerus succeeded, but fell under the spell of her twin sister, who used the same name, Bacchis. Mnesilochus, coming home, and hearing of this, is not unnaturally led to believe that the girl he loves has become the mistress of his friend. Before this he had intended to buy her release from a contract to a soldier, entered into before he had met her. His slave Chrysalus had made this possible for him by telling his father a false story explaining that they had been obliged to leave the money in Ephesus.

Plautus has changed the names of these three characters; in Menander Mnesilochus was Sostratos, Pistoclerus was Moschos, and Chrysalus was Syros. Sostratos, left alone after hearing of what he supposes to be his friend's disloyalty, reflects as follows:

> He's gone then ...[1] She'll keep her hold on him. You made Sostratos your prey first.—She'll deny it, no doubt about that; she's brazen enough; every god in heaven will be brought into it. A curse on that wicked woman! (*Makes for the door of the house in which she is.*) Back, Sostratos! She may talk you over. I've been her slave (?) ... but let her use her persuasion on me when my pockets are empty and I've got nothing. I'll give my father all the money. She'll stop making herself attractive when she finds herself telling her tale to a dead man, as the proverb has it. I must go to him at once.

At this moment the father returns from the market and Sostratos tells him that there was no truth in the story spun

[1] A few words are lost, indicated here by dots. Perhaps 'you'll keep your hold'.

by Syrus: 'forget it, and come with me to get the money.'
The pair go off into the town, where it must have been left,
and the act ends.

How did Plautus deal with this?

> Whether I should now believe my friend and companion
> or Bacchis to be my greater enemy, is a big problem. Did
> she prefer him? Let her have him! Excellent! I'll say she's
> done herself no good by that. Let no one ever take me
> for a prophet if I don't absolutely and completely—love
> her! I'll see to it that she can't say she got hold of a man
> she could laugh at; I'll go home—and steal something
> from my father to give her! I'll be revenged on her one
> way or another and make a beggar of—my father! But
> am I really in my right mind when I talk like this about
> what is still in the future? I love her, I think, if there's
> anything I can be sure of, but I'd rather outbeggar any
> beggar than let her get a featherweight of gold from my
> money. My God, she shan't have the laugh of me! I've
> decided to hand over all the gold to my father. So then
> she'll coax me when my pockets are empty and I've no
> resources, when it will mean as little to me as if she were
> telling tales to a dead man at his grave. It's quite decided
> that I give the gold back to my father.

Adding that he will prevail on his father not to be angry with
Chrysalus, he goes in. Menander's scene between father and
son has disappeared. Plautus had to make some cuts to
compensate for his expansions, and this he thought he could
dispense with. He must have observed that Nicobulus, as the
father is called in his play, had earlier gone to the forum and
had not yet come back, but perhaps he hoped that the spectators would not notice.

Menander allowed it to be understood from Sostratos' words
that he still felt the girl's attraction—'she may talk you over'.
Plautus makes it explicit in a sentence striking for its unexpected termination: 'if I don't absolutely and completely——'
the context suggests 'ruin her', but surprisingly the conclusion
is 'love her'. Pleased with this device, he repeats it twice, to
produce jests that do not suit Mnesilochus' character but

drive home the point that he is still prepared to put the girl before his father. His infatuation is then confirmed, for the slowest hearer, 'I love her'. That is an avowal that Sostratos did not make; anger was uppermost in his mind. After declaring his love Mnesilochus expresses a determination not to let Bacchis get her hands on any of his money; this resolve is inadequately explained.

Plautus also modifies the purpose of the young man's action over the money. Sostratos thought of the effect on the girl: she would have no use for a poor man. Mnesilochus, whose whole speech is self-centred, thinks of himself; if he has nothing, he will be unable to respond to her wiles. Almost all that Sostratos said was concerned with how *she* would behave. The same preoccupation with her and her thoughts coloured a second soliloquy, which he delivered in the next act. He came back with his father, who left once again; then he broke out:

Yes, I believe I should enjoy seeing this perfect lady, this love of mine now that my pockets are empty, making herself attractive and expecting—'rightaway' she says to herself—all the money I'm bringing her. 'O, yes, he's bringing it all right, generously by heaven—could anyone be more generous?—and don't I deserve it?' She has turned out well enough to be exactly what I once thought her—one can be thankful for that—and I pity that fool Moschos. In one way I'm angry, but on the other hand I don't reckon he's responsible for the wrong I've been done, but that woman, who's the most brazenfaced of the lot of them.

With that Moschos came impatiently out of the house where the two sisters were.

Moschos. Then if he's heard I'm here, where on earth is he?—Oh, welcome, Sostratos.
Sostratos. (*sulkily*) Welcome.
Moschos. Why so downcast and gloomy? And the hint of a tear in your look? You've not found some unexpected trouble here?

PLAUTUS

Sostratos. Yes.

Moschos. Then aren't you going to tell me?

Sostratos. It's in the house, Moschos, you know.

Moschos. What do you mean?

Sostratos. [*A sentence is lost.*] That's the first wrong you've done me.

Moschos. I? Wronged you? Heaven forbid, Sostratos.

Sostratos. I didn't expect it, either.

Moschos. What are you talking about?

Here the papyrus ends, but it seems probable that the misunderstanding was rapidly cleared up.

Plautus, who had no chorus to cover a lapse of time, could not plausibly make Mnesilochus return instantly after going off to give his father the gold and to explain away the slave's story. Instead he advanced the entry of Pistoclerus. No sooner has Mnesilochus gone in than his friend comes out from the other house, into which he directs his opening words:

> Your instructions, Bacchis, shall take first place ahead of all else; I'm to look out for Mnesilochus and bring him back here to you in my company. Indeed, if my message has reached him, it's a puzzle what can be delaying him. I'll go and call here, in case he's at home.

Moschos did not babble like this nor did he need instructions from Bacchis; his single entrance line expresses his own eagerness to meet his long-absent old friend. Pistoclerus' laboured explanations provide, even if it be inadequately, for a passage of time during which Mnesilochus may be supposed to have dealt with his father. So he can now emerge, and Plautus continues, summarising events since the end of Menander's act.

> *Mnesilochus.* I've returned my father all the gold. I'd like her to meet me now, now that my pockets are empty, she who despises me. But how reluctantly my father pardoned Chrysalus when I asked! But I did finally prevail on him not to harbour any anger.
> *Pistoclerus.* Is this my friend?
> *Mnesilochus.* Is this my enemy I see?

131

Pistoclerus. It is, to be sure.

Mnesilochus. It is he. I will go up and meet him face to face.

Pistoclerus. Welcome to you, Mnesilochus.

Mnesilochus. And to you.

Pistoclerus. Let us have a dinner to celebrate your safe return from foreign parts.

Mnesilochus. I've no liking for a dinner that will make me sick!

Pistoclerus. You don't say that you have been faced with something to upset you on your return?

Mnesilochus. Yes, and a very violent upset.

Pistoclerus. What caused it?

Mnesilochus. A man I previously thought my friend.

Pistoclerus. There are many men alive today who act in that manner and that fashion. When you count them as friends, they are found to be false in their falsity, busy with their tongues, but sluggish in service and light in loyalty. There is not a soul whose success they do not envy; but their inactivity makes it sure enough that no one envies them.

Mnesilochus. I'll swear that you've studied their ways well and have a good grip on them. But there is one thing more: their bad character brings them bad luck; they have no friends and make enemies all round. And in their folly they reckon they are cheating others, when they are really cheating themselves. That is how it is with the man I thought as good a friend to me as I am to myself. He took all the pains in his power to do me any harm he could and to get everything that belonged to me into his own hands.[1]

Pistoclerus. He must be a wicked man.

Mnesilochus. I think so.

---

[1] This speech and the previous one were omitted in some manuscripts of late antiquity and it is disputed whether they are by Plautus—if so, they may have been a second thought on his part, since their removal leaves no gap—or whether they were inserted by someone else for a revival of the play. Whatever the truth of this may be, the moralising lines were expected to win the approval of a second-century audience.

Pistoclerus. Speak out, I beg you, tell me who he is.
Mnesilochus. One who wishes you well. Otherwise I
would pray you to do him any harm you could.
Pistoclerus. Just say who the man is. If I don't hurt him
somehow, call me the worst of slackers.
Mnesilochus. The man's a rogue, but he's a friend of yours.
Pistoclerus. The more reason for telling me who he is. I
don't care much for the friendship of a rogue.
Mnesilochus. I see that I can't do anything but tell you
his name. Pistoclerus, you have utterly ruined me, your
friend.

Menander made Moschos see at once that something was
wrong, just as an intimate friend would, and Sostratos was
quickly brought to explain his resentment. For Plautus this
was missing an opportunity; he could use a motif that he may
well have met in some other play. If Mnesilochus were to denounce the man he supposed to have injured him, but without
giving his name, Pistoclerus with nothing on his conscience
could be made to speak unwittingly in his own condemnation,
and Mnesilochus could be made to lead him on. (More accur-
ately, Pistoclerus condemns not himself, but the man whom his
friend supposes him to be.) Plautus' scene is somewhat contrived, but it might be effective on the stage, as the audience
enjoyed Pistoclerus' repeated failures to understand. One
should not condemn it for not being Menander's; its explicit
vigour will have made it more attractive to the Roman
audience than his would have been. But it must be realised
that Menander conceived the young men quite differently.
His Moschos is sensitive and direct, immediately perceives
the other's distress, and would not meet it with four pompous
lines of generalisation about false friends; Sostratos, although
not unresentful, does not see an enemy in Moschos, but puts
the blame on the girl, not on his old companion. Plautus
worked with stock motifs, Menander with lifelike figures of his
own invention.

Now that it is possible to compare a passage of Menander
with Plautus' version, there is proof that in his later works at
least the Latin dramatist dealt very freely with his original.
It was not just a matter of inserting extraneous jokes into a

more or less faithfully translated text. Scholars had realised that there must have been changes when a *canticum* (see p. 120) replaced a spoken scene, but not that a scene could remain spoken yet be given a new form. We now know that he could refashion both monologue and dialogue which were essential to the progress of the plot, making the new version do all that was necessary to carry the play forward, but substituting his own characterisation.

The result of this new evidence must be to show that greater difficulty than some have imagined must attend any effort to work back from Plautus to the Greek play he adapted. On the other hand since the failure to account for the movements of the father is proved to be due to him and not to Menander, there is support for those who think such imperfections reliable clues to Plautine workmanship. But although he is here convicted of carelessness, there is new proof of his independence; it seems he is to be credited with responsibility for a greater part of his plays than some scholars have supposed.

8

Terence

PUBLIUS Terentius Afer was believed by later Romans to have been born at Carthage, brought to Rome as a slave, and given a liberal education by his owner, Terentius Lucanus, who soon set him free. They may have had good reason for this belief, or the story may have grown from his name. Afer means a member of the dark native races of North Africa; an African would be a slave, and a manumitted slave took the middle name of his master. But the name Afer does not of necessity indicate a place of origin or a servile birth; it is attested as a Roman family name. If Terence did come from Africa, the excellence of his Latin is noteworthy but not unparalleled; Livius Andronicus, the father of Latin literature, was a Greek; Caecilius, the leading writer of comedy when Terence was young, is said to have been a slave from Gaul. Men who have won literary fame in languages not their own are not common in the modern world, but some can be named.

In his own lifetime Terence was charged with having received help in his dramatic work from friends who belonged to the best families. In the prologue to his last play, *Adelphoe* (*Brothers*), he wrote:

> Those ill-wishers say that men of famous families help him and constantly write along with him. They think this a violent aspersion, but he regards it as the height of praise if he is approved by men who have your unanimous approval, and that of the people too, men whose services everyone has on occasion used in war, in peace, in business.

This is typically elusive and evasive. Terence neither admits the charge nor denies it. If he had confessed it to be true, as it may well have been, it might have been thought that he had but a small share in the dramas which went under his name, that he was a mere front for some nobles; if it were false and he had declared it so, the great men involved might not have welcomed their loss of literary glory, however undeserved.

Later it became widely believed that these men included the younger Scipio and Gaius Laelius, and ignorance of the fact that he was not their junior allowed the scandalous suggestion that their motive was pederasty. This charge may be dismissed, but a literary association need not attract the same disbelief. Terence's plays were produced in the years 166 to 160, when Scipio was about eighteen to twenty-four years of age. It is by no means unlikely that the young aristocrat, interested in Greek culture, should have dabbled in playwriting, although he would not have wished to be thought a professional dramatist, or that Terence, for anything we know not very much older, should have accepted his collaboration and patronage.

It must be emphasised, however, that very probably ancient guess-work invented the connection with Scipio and his friends; no reliable evidence seems to have survived, since one Santra, probably a contemporary of Cicero's, suggested a trio of older personages, arguing that if Terence had needed help, he would not have gone to men younger than himself. Nevertheless the accepted guess may have been sound, it may have been supported by oral tradition, and it may also be significant that *Adelphoe*, the prologue to which mentions these alleged collaborators, was performed at the funeral games of L. Aemilius Paullus, and Scipio organised those.

In any case the support of powerful men, whoever they were, with literary interests, would make it easier to understand the nature of Terence's plays, which make few concessions to popular taste. When he began to write, less than thirty years had passed since the death of Plautus, and it would not seem that the majority of the audience had greatly changed. The first two performances of *Hecyra* (*The Mother-in-Law*) were failures, and the prologue to the third, spoken by the leading actor, Turpio, explains why:

> Once again I am bringing you *The Mother-in-Law*, a play I have never been allowed to act in silence; disaster has swamped it. Your appreciation, if it can be allied to our efforts, will put an end to that disaster. On the first

occasion when I began to act it, the great renown of some
boxers (expectation of a tight-rope walker was thrown in),
friends getting together, a clatter of conversation, women's
penetrating voices, made me leave the theatre all too
soon . . . I brought it on again: the first act was liked, and
then there came a rumour that gladiators were on the
programme; the people came flocking in, rioting and
shouting, fighting for places: when that happened, I
could not keep *my* place.

Yet, unlike Plautus, Terence made almost no attempt to
put in something for everybody in his audience. His plays
give the impression of being what spectators ought to like
rather than what they would enjoy. Although there are more
long lines spoken to the music of the pipe than in Menander,
the songs in varied metres, which had diversified the plays of
Plautus and seem still to have been used by Caecilius, are no
longer present. There are no indecencies, no puns, no slang-
ing-matches, no gloatings over corporal punishments. Instead
there is concentrated action, moving steadily forward, and
dialogue that is often rapid and generally needs unremitting
attention if the thread is not to be lost. Terence's plays re-
semble those of Menander rather than those of Plautus. In
fact four of his six are adaptations of Menandrean originals and
the other two are taken from Apollodorus of Carystus, a less-
gifted follower of the great Athenian.

Anyone who wished to argue that Terence was not over-
taxing the capability of his public might appeal to the fact
that Caecilius had already shown a similar preference for plays
by Menander. But so far as we can see, he was not true to
Menander's spirit. Aulus Gellius, a writer of miscellanies in
the second century AD, compares three pairs of passages by
the two authors and exclaims at Caecilius' lack of taste. In
one the Latin author introduces the old joke that the husband
of a rich wife wishes her dead, and makes him imagine her
boasting to her contemporaries and relatives that she has in
her old age forced her husband to give up his young mistress,
a thing *they* could not have done when they were still in their
first youth; in another he causes the husband's friend to crack
a coarse jest about her bad breath, wishing to raise a laugh, so

Gellius says, more than to provide words suitable for the character. Gellius accuses him of descending to the level of the mime. Caecilius' changes were not merely a matter of adding familiar motifs that would appeal to the more simple-minded. In these passages, at least, he dealt freely with the Greek, with which he kept no more than a minimal necessary relation. He seems to have felt no commitment to maintain a colloquial style: other fragments show that he often made great use of alliteration, a device which must have had a popular appeal, much as early drama in England used rhyme, still found in parts of our pantomimes.

Terence on the other hand attempted to transfer Menander to the Roman stage without changes and additions obviously inconsistent with the qualities of the Greek. In his prologues he speaks of 'literary art' and tells the spectators that they have a chance of 'bringing distinction to the dramatic festival'. But his admiration for Menander did not make him rest content with mere translation. Virgil was to be credited with the epigram that it was easier to steal his club from Hercules than a line from Homer; but it was his ambition not only to borrow from Homer but to improve on him wherever he could. Similarly Terence may have been aware that he could not hope to reproduce all Menander's merits, but he could try in some ways to better him.

The most obvious of his changes, and one which must have immediately struck anyone who knew the original plays, was to abandon the convention of the expository prologue. He retained a prologue, but used it for quite different purposes. Spoken by an actor, perhaps always by the principal actor, in his own person, not that of the character he was to represent, it gives the name of the play, as had been done in some of the Plautine prologues; twice Menander is mentioned as the original author, but once it is said that there is no need to name either the dramatist or the man he is translating, since the majority of the audience will already know. Presumably the minority, if it was a minority, did not care. But the greater part of the prologue is given over to a defence of Terence's use of his originals and to counter-attacks on a critic, an older writer of comedies; he is not named, but can be identified as one Luscius from Lanuvium.

An earlier move towards making the prologue a place for literary criticism has been seen in a fragment from some Greek author in which the god Dionysus complains of long-winded deities who set out all the facts, which the spectators fail to take in. He then proceeds to what promises to be a detailed exposition of the background to his play; the contrast between his theory and his practice is amusing. But it was Terence who took the decisive step of separating the prologue from the play and expressing in it seriously meant views on dramatic methods. This was to have long-lasting effects in the European theatre. One may compare the prologues to Ben Jonson's *Volpone* or *Every Man in His Humour*. Even when there is nothing more than mere *captatio benevolentiae*, as in Dekker's *Shoemaker's Holiday*, or witty trifling, as in Goldsmith's *She Stoops to Conquer*, a line of descent goes back to Terence, who established this form of independent introduction.

In the prologue to *Andria* (*A Woman from Andros*), which is based on Menander's play of the same title, he says that he had been attacked by his older rival for transferring to it matter from Menander's *Perinthia* (*A Woman from Perinthos*); his critics maintain that plays should not be 'spoiled' or 'adulterated'. He replies that he has the precedent of Naevius, Plautus and Ennius, whose 'negligence' he prefers to rival rather than the 'obscure carefulness' of the critics. It seems that he charges them with practising a fidelity to their models of which the public, who were not students of Greek drama, could not be aware, while they accuse him of spoiling plays by introducing foreign matter. He defends himself by declaring that his predecessors had also adulterated their plays.

A play may be 'adulterated' in various ways; he had done it in a particular manner, that of blending parts of two different comedies to make a new one.[1] So far as *Andria* is concerned, the fourth-century scholar Donatus was unable to identify much borrowing from *Perinthia*, but in two other plays also, *Eunuchus* and *Adelphoe*, Terence adopted this procedure of blending two originals, as their prologues explain. Its effects are clearly visible in both but they are easier to understand in the latter. In

---

[1] Some modern scholars use the word for adulteration, *con-taminatio*, in this restricted sense, as a technical term.

Menander's play the young hero had before it opened abducted a girl from a slave-trader on behalf of his brother, who loved her. Terence found in a play by Diphilus a lively scene of just such an abduction, which Plautus in his adaptation had for some reason omitted. He decided to enliven his play by using this scene, translated (so he unconvincingly alleges) word for word, to represent by stage-action what was only narrated in Menander.

This involved him in various difficulties. First, Diphilus' scene was enacted outside the slave-trader's house at the moment of the theft; his efforts to prevent it very naturally led to violence. In the play of Menander, and therefore in that of Terence, the slaver's lodging was not represented on the stage, so the scene had to be transferred to the street outside the house of the young man, whose raiding party he had followed. This necessitated some alterations of wording, but even so the exchanges remain more suitable to the earlier occasion. Secondly, Terence was obliged to introduce this scene after the opening monologue, which leads into a duologue where the young men's father indignantly reports that the theft has become the talk of the town. Clearly he cannot have learned this before the son had had time to bring the girl home; there is an absurdity in the time-sequence, which had to be ignored.

Thirdly, by causing the slaver to follow on the heels of the raiding party, Terence brings him to the young man's house before he is needed there by the plot of Menander's play, and he has to stand about, awkwardly forgotten, during scenes of explanation between the two brothers. There is perhaps a fourth point. The scene taken from Diphilus ends with an assertion by the young man that the girl is really a free woman and no slave. Nothing more is heard of this, and it is not clear whether Terence, unwilling to abandon a fine climax, left a loose end, or whether he believed it would be understood that the claim was a false one and no more than a move to embarrass her owner.

This will serve to illustrate the difficulties which may beset the transference of a scene from one play to another. Nevertheless at one time many scholars believed that it had been extensively practised by Plautus. He was even supposed to have fused whole plays together, to make one Latin play out of two Greek. Today some hold that he cannot be proved ever to have resorted to either device. Certainly he 'adulterated' his originals by adding matter of his own invention; this kind of adulteration was not that for which Terence was reprehended, and Terence may be suspected of disingenuously sheltering behind him. Yet one need not deny that Plautus may well have found inspiration for some of his supplements in plays other than the one he was at the moment adapting, even if what he acquired was a suggestion rather than a model to be translated.

Terence's reasons for giving up the expository prologue are unknown, and no more can be done than speculate about them. Perhaps he found it unrealistic to make a character unashamedly explain the opening situation to the audience. But that is not altogether convincing, since in *Adelphoe*, his last play, much of the exposition is contained in a long opening monologue composed as an address to the audience, not as a piece of reflection; and he shows no objection to narrative monologues in the body of his plays. Perhaps he thought that more was to be gained by allowing the spectators to share the characters' surprise as facts were brought to light than by giving them a superior comprehensive view from the first. Either way of writing is defensible; each of the two forms of drama brings its own gains and losses. But it is to be noticed that the Terentian method of construction has predominated in the theatre ever since his day.

It is however one thing to write an original play in this manner, another to convert a drama written in the other way to the new fashion. In so far as an expository prologue contained information about the background necessary to make the characters' actions intelligible, this had to be conveyed, when the prologue was dropped, to the audience in some other way. On the whole Terence solved the problem not unskilfully; he succeeded in introducing explanations where they were needed.

Terence had a way with personal names that may be seen as significant of his relation to his models. Most are known from Greek New Comedy, and almost all are suitable for use over and over again. In fact Terence duplicated even more than Menander had done; in his six plays there are three old men called Chremes, three hetairai called Bacchis, three married women called Sostrata. Yet he seems regularly to have replaced the name in the Greek original by a new one. Thus he at once declared his adherence to Greek dramatic methods and his own originality in handling his models.

A complete picture of the changes he made is impossible because so little detail is known of the Greek plays he adapted. A very little is given by Donatus and something can be deduced from study of his plays' structure and knowledge of Menander's methods of writing. But there are several cases where his object can be divined; it was to enrich the original material by additions that were Greek in spirit, sometimes taken from a Greek play, but likely to have a popular appeal. It has been seen how the *Adelphoe* gained a scene of lively action and some rough-and-tumble; let us consider the other two Menandrean dramas to which additions are certain.

Andria has a young man, Pamphilus, who is in love with a poor unprotected girl, Glycerium, but whom his father wishes to marry a neighbour's daughter, Philumena. He consents to this match, believing there to be an obstacle which will prevent it. Terence added a motif, perhaps of his own invention, perhaps taken from some other play, in the shape of a youth who is Pamphilus' friend and who loves Philumena. His jealousy is an easily understood emotion and the extra complication for Pamphilus provides the spectators with a further source of interest. This is a more likely way to explain the addition than Donatus' suggestion that it was done to avoid disappointment for Philumena (who never appears on the stage) when Glycerium turns out to be another daughter of the neighbour and so an eligible bride for Pamphilus.

The most pervasive additions are those made to *Eunuchus*, where there have been introduced the figures of Thraso and Gnatho, a soldier and his parasite, taken on Terence's own admission from *Kolax*, another play by Menander, which had a totally different plot. Thraso is made the rival of a rich young man, Phaedria, for a courtesan, Thais, and replaces some other rival, perhaps a less colourful soldier, perhaps a merchant, in Menander's *Eunuchos*. But Gnatho makes an additional character, except inasmuch as at his first entrance he replaces a slave who brought the 'heroine' to Thais' house as a gift from the rival. His entrance monologue, describing his technique of flattery, is very amusing, but the entertainment is bought at the expense of letting his charge stand about in the street with nothing to do while he delivers it.

A second amusing scene is provided by the sixty lines with which Thraso makes his first entrance. More than half of this has no connection with the plot of *Eunuchus*, but exemplifies his tasteless boasting, to which he is egged on by the malicious Gnatho, whose irony he is too stupid to understand. This is certainly based on material taken from *Kolax*, although it cannot be determined how closely that play was followed. Although the latter part of the scene continues the same manner and characterisation, it is essential to the plot: Thraso boorishly invites Thais to dinner and Gnatho suggests to him a method of making her jealous which the audience will know to be certain to cause her great embarrassment; Gnatho is clever enough to guess that it will be very unwelcome to her. This must be Terence's composition, even if he was able to find some material for it in Menander's plays.

In the following passage Phaedria's slave brings Thais his master's gift of a slave-girl and a eunuch. Unknown to Phaedria, his younger brother has substituted himself disguised for the eunuch. Terence has made changes here, necessitated by the removal of the rival of Menander's *Eunuchos*, whose place is taken by Thraso and Gnatho. Their extent is not to be determined, but one exchange is undoubtedly based on *Kolax*: Gnatho suddenly bursts out laughing, and when asked why, replies that he had just thought of the soldier's quip at the expense of a man from Rhodes; this had been mentioned in the earlier part of the previous scene, and was an adaptation of a joke preserved in a fragment of that play.

Thraso and Gnatho next appear in the 'siege-scene', where an abortive move is made to storm Thais' house in order to recover the soldier's gift to her. This again is not only amusing, as the parasite's malice and the soldier's cowardice interact, but also has lively action on the stage, as the 'troops', who consist of four slaves, are disposed. Some of the material may be taken from *Kolax*; that is no more than a guess, but it is certain that this scene is a lively replacement of some less noisy attempt at recovery in Menander's *Eunuchos*.

The two characters from *Kolax* are seen again at the end of the play. Gnatho arranges a pact between Phaedria and the soldier that they should share Thais' favours; it will be an effect of this that it will be the soldier who pays. Phaedria agrees moreover that Gnatho should transfer to his patronage. Although the matter is disputed, I have no doubt that those are right who see here a Terentian ending. In the earlier part of the play Phaedria has been portrayed as intensely jealous of Thraso, and Thais has promised to abandon the soldier so soon as she has secured the 'heroine', whom she hopes to restore to her parents. The pact is brutally inconsistent with this relation between them; moreover it utterly disregards the position of Thais. She is an independent and good-hearted courtesan, sincerely concerned to reunite the girl with her family, although not without self-interest, since she hopes that in their gratitude they will take her under their protection; this protection she has now attained. It is absurd that she should be disposed of behind her back, as if she were a slave, and condemned to the embraces of the ridiculous soldier, in order that Phaedria should enjoy her for nothing. It is a minor absurdity that he should saddle himself with the support of the dangerous Gnatho.

Very possibly this ending was taken from *Kolax*, where Thraso's rival in love was, unlike Phaedria, an impecunious young man, and the object of their attentions a slave, whose inclinations it may not have been necessary to consult. Terence's belief that the conclusion he gave to his *Eunuchus* would be welcomed by the Roman audience, who would enjoy its ingenuity, the soldier's foolish acceptance of a bad bargain, and the young man's combination of success with economy, is based on a difference between Greek and Roman society. In Terence's time at least the *meretrix* had an opprobrious name, and was despised and tolerated as a necessary evil; the Greek hetaira must not be sentimentalised, but by her name she was 'a companion' and she was accepted as a useful member of the community. The best kind of hetaira, of which Thais is one, could be a woman of some wealth, an independent mind and self-respect. This was something not understood at Rome.

Another play the end of which some think Terence adapted in an attempt to meet Roman taste is *Adelphoe*; I believe them to be right. The theme is that of a contrast between two methods of bringing up a son, the one permissive, the other restrictive. Neither proves to be entirely successful but Micio, the father who practises the former method, is, until the last act, presented in a favourable light as generous, realistic and humane; when he has occasion to give his son an understanding reproof, the young man accepts it and reflects that their relation is more like that of brothers or friends than that usual between father and son, and determines to do nothing that would be against his wishes. The other father, his brother, who is harsh and without joy in life, finds himself in ridiculous situations and is at a loss when faced with a moral problem over which Micio has no hesitation: although it is not the match he would have chosen, he never doubts that his son should marry the poor girl whom he loves and who has borne him a child.

In the last act this martinet declares in a monologue that he sees that indulgence is the way to win popularity and that he will adopt that course for the brief spell of life that is left him. He proceeds in some amusing scenes to practise a new-found affability and generosity, not at his own expense but at that of his brother, whom he provides with a widow as a wife. In Terence's play the permissive parent feebly resists, but is so accustomed to letting people have their way that he has to accept this bride. Donatus remarks that in Menander he raised no objection to the marriage, and if he did not resist this, the heaviest of all the demands made on him, it is unlikely that he made any difficulties about any of the others, none of which are unreasonable. In Terence his ineffective objections are designed to show a lack of will.

Finally his brother says that the object of his apparent change of character was to show that the other's popularity did not depend on what was right and good and a true way of life, but on complaisance and indulgence. He offers himself as one with the knowledge to reprehend, correct, and where suitable support the young; thereupon the permissively educated son declares that he will accept his guidance. Although Molière, Lessing and Goethe all felt that this ending was wrong, orthodoxy interprets it as supporting the view that the right form of education is a mean between the strict and the permissive. However much this may appeal to those who subscribe to that view, I do not believe that this was the play's intended message. The reason for the martinet's change of front must be given by the monologue; it was to win popularity. It is a dramatic necessity that the speaker of a monologue utters what he believes to be the truth. What he here says is quite inconsistent with putting on an act for a short time with the intention of exposing the weakness of his brother's way of life. It follows that Terence has altered the balance of the end of the play, to bring down the scales on the side of the man whose stern hard-working parsimonious austerity accorded more with Roman ideals than did his easy-going life-enjoying brother.

Other ways in which Terence enriched Menander were comparatively superficial. In *Eunuchus* the stage was made fuller by dividing a single part into two characters, Pythias and Dorias,[1] and in other plays a character is sometimes kept on after the point at which he must have left in the Greek. Breaking of the three-actor rule (see p. 78) together with the fact that he takes no substantial part in the second scene is the evidence for this change. Sometimes his continued presence allows him to overhear a monologue by someone else, a situation which Terence not infrequently contrives.

He also tried to reduce the number of non-speakers on the stage. Slaves, who in a Greek play would be given orders which they carried out in silence, are by him allowed a line or two. It is hard to say whether the motive was realism or simply a desire to make the scene more lively. He has been credited with realism, but on insufficient grounds. If, as Donatus seems to have believed but many modern scholars deny, he introduced Antipho into *Eunuchus* to provide a hearer for the young man's account of the rape he had perpetrated in his disguise as a eunuch, the reason was not a dislike on principle of monologues, which are of frequent occurrence. Perhaps he felt it to

---

[1] This is not universally accepted.

be unsuitable for the transgressor to confide directly to the audience what many of them must regard as a crime.

Nowhere can the words of Terence be compared with any extended passage of a Greek model; this prevents appreciation of the changes he made in the details of language. He seems to have broken speeches up, made the exchanges more rapid and multiplied interjections. What can be done is to observe how he differs from Plautus and even Caecilius.

Plautus exploited the natural genius of Latin for assonance, alliteration and full-blown, almost tautological, expression. Terence set to work with remarkable success to reproduce the merits of Menander's style, its simplicity, flexibility and concision, although Latin was an inadequate instrument for this purpose, having a limited vocabulary, if vulgar words were excluded, and a restricted ability to express nuances. Terence was praised by Julius Caesar as a 'lover of pure speech'. 'Pure speech' was that practised by the conventional educated upper classes, and may have been the nearest equivalent to Menander's standard in Greek. Terence used this kind of Latin with great skill, making next to no use of foreign words, and attaining speed by his brevity. Not only did he avoid repetitiousness, he often truncated sentences by leaving out a verb or a subject which could be understood, or could even reduce them to a single word.

The result is admirable and Caesar could compare him with Menander; but he called him a 'Menander halved', and regretted that he lacked 'power' or 'force' (*uis*), and spoke of his 'gentle' writings. What this means is perhaps that his writing is too equable, it lacks the ebb and flow which gives life to the Greek poet's writing and enables him to mirror every kind of emotion.

Epilogue

THE last recorded Roman revival of a play by Plautus, his *Pseudolus*, took place in the time of Cicero and, although it is dangerous to argue from silence, it is probable enough that in subsequent centuries he had more attention from grammarians than from actors. But Quintilian, writing about AD 90, mentions some comic actors as if their names were well known and implies that they appeared, wearing masks, in plays by Terence. It is possible that under the Empire Terence was more frequently revived than our very scanty sources reveal, although new comedies were by then written only occasionally and for the study rather than the stage. Some of his medieval manuscripts have illustrations of scenes performed by masked actors; these may be derived from an unknown artist of the fourth century, who may himself, however, never have seen a performance but have adapted earlier drawings. Donatus, if he can be believed, says that in his time (*c.* 350) female parts in Terence were played by actresses without masks.

But there can be no doubt that at Rome the predominant kind of play became that presented by actors of mime, which abandoned any claim to literary merit. Even in the days of Plautus and Terence a large part of the audience had simple unrefined tastes, which were not satisfied by their dramas. In the time of Augustus Horace alleges that the uneducated and stupid who form the majority will in the middle of a play demand a bear or boxers, for that is what the masses enjoy. Under the Empire their tastes seem to have been catered for. The performances of the mimic actors, who were never admitted to the guilds of the Artists of Dionysus, were despised by the cultivated writers who mention them, so that there is not much evidence. They seem to have been varied, ranging from turns and sketches to plays made of successive scenes, in which frequent elements were songs, dirty jokes, deceived husbands, poisons, sleeping-draughts and trained animals, that certain recipe for theatrical success.

Yet if the mime was victorious on the stage, Terence was important in education. Boys were made to read him for his Latinity and his moral sentiments, while the impropriety of many actions done by his characters was conveniently overlooked. As Christianity spread, the less bigoted found themselves obliged to adopt the pagan system of education and to approve reading of the standard authors. We find Terence quoted by Saints Jerome and Augustine and other Fathers of the Church, although it may often be suspected that their knowledge of his lines came from anthologies rather than study of the plays.

The theatre itself, however, was widely condemned, both in the West and in the East. The denunciations show that what their authors had in mind was primarily the mime, but comedies were seen as tarred with the same brush. For Tertullian they were 'instigators of lust, licentious and prodigal; we should not accept when it is spoken what we abhor when it is done'. Presumably some Christians were caused to abstain from theatre-going, but many continued to attend. The disappearance of comedy from the stage was due to a lowering of educational standards rather than to the Church.

Terence continued to be copied and read during the Middle Ages. A dialogue composed perhaps in the seventh century and certainly not later than the ninth confronts him with a detractor, to whom he replies that he is loved by all. In the ninth century the nun Hrosvitha of Gandersheim was distressed that those who delighted in the sweetness of his language should be sullied by learning of wickedness; she offered a substitute in plays of her own composition, written in clear and vigorous prose, which celebrated 'the praiseworthy chastity of holy virgins' instead of 'the disgraceful lewdness of lascivious women'.

At the revival of learning Terence was printed, acted and translated. There were at least 446 complete editions between 1470 and 1600, mainly in Italy and France. Acting seems to have occurred principally in schools, where he was used in the teaching of Latin, even at first in Jesuit schools, although he was soon banned there. Performances took place in Italy as early as 1476; Luther did not object to the practice in Germany, and in England the boys of St Paul's School recited *Phormio* before Cardinal Wolsey in 1528 and those of Westminster School acted plays of Terence before Queen Elizabeth in 1569. The performance of Terence in Latin became, and still is, a regular event at Westminster. The first complete translation into English was by a Puritan clergyman, R. Bernard (1598); Macchiavelli translated *Andria* into Italian and Ariosto *Andria*, *Eunuchus* and *Phormio*.

Plautus also became known, but a little later than Terence and less widely. Particularly in France he was unappreciated. Montaigne, who loved Terence, found him vulgar. He better suited the more robust taste of the English. Francis Meres declared in 1598 that Plautus was accounted 'the best for Comedy among the Latines' (*Palladis Tamia: Wits Treasury*, p. xv).

Far more important than revivals and translations were the new vernacular comedies which Plautus and Terence inspired. Although they at first made use of material from the Latin plays, their writers contributed much of their own invention. It is significant that whereas Plautus left his plays in their original Greek setting, they normally transferred them to their own country, and this new situation encouraged originality. Shakespeare, it is true, allowed his *Comedy of Errors*, based on Plautus' *Menaechmi*, to remain in a Greek city, but he enlarged the plot not only by material from the *Amphitruo*, which contributed the idea of indistinguishable servants of indistinguishable masters, but also in other ways, such as the development of the character of the wife Luciana and the introduction of the merchant Balthasar, both with non-Greek names. Perhaps the most important change was to imbed the story of the twin Menaechmi in the framework of that of Aegeon, in peril of his life when the play opens, freed and restored to his wife when it ends. This strikes a note of seriousness which can be heard from time to time in the comic centre of this play also.

But forty years earlier *Ralph Roister Doister* (*c.* 1553), by Nicholas Udall, the Headmaster of Westminster School, already adjusts figures borrowed from *Miles Gloriosus* and *Eunuchus* to suit their new place in English society, although the parasite's name, Merrygreek, reveals his origins, and by adding

151

other native figures makes something that genuinely reflects English life.

Although the vernacular writers had a fertile inventiveness which quickly carried them away from their classical ancestors, they learnt from them at least three lessons, without which modern drama would not have come into being. The first was to write in prose. Because the prosody of Plautus and Terence was not the familiar prosody of later poetry, but a better reflection of the phonetic facts of Latin speech, it was not recognised in the sixteenth century that they had written in verse. Freed by this misapprehension from the restraints of metre and of rhyme, the writer of comedy could develop a style which the flexible rhythms of prose made possible.

The second lesson was to treat the characters as individual human beings and not as the allegorical figures or exponents of abstract themes which they had been in medieval plays. The third lesson, as important as the second, was how to construct a plot, how to make scenes not merely succeed one another but grow one from another, and how to impose form upon a play by act-divisions which correspond to stages in the development of the story. This is what the ancient writers of comedy had to teach those who were setting that form of drama on a new course.

Appendix

Some Problems Concerning Old Comedy

1. Was there any scene-painting?

Aristotle believed that Sophocles (died 406/5) introduced *skenographia* (literally 'painting of the *skene*') *Poetics* 1449 a 18. Although this could mean no more than the painting of a permanent background, perhaps architectural, on the façade of the stage-building, that seems an improbable explanation, since such an innovation would have brought an equal benefit to his competitors, or at least to those whose plays were set before a palace or temple; it might have been resented by those who had imagined a setting in an army camp or on a solitary shore. Hence many have supposed that movable screens, on which a suitable background was painted, were placed against the *skene*.

Even if this was done in tragedy, it does not follow that such painted scenery was used in Aristophanes' comedies, or that it would have had any value there. Whereas tragedy usually observed the 'unity of place', Old Comedy is not so bound, but its action shifts location without apology and with the inconsequence of a dream. So *The Acharnians* opens in the Pnyx, then is outside Dikaiopolis' house in the country, then outside that of Euripides in the city, then in a private market-place, then outside the houses of Dikaiopolis and Lamachus. There is no opportunity for changing scenery to suit the different places, and no need for scenery; in fact things are better left to the spectators' imagination. Similar considerations will apply to most of Aristophanes' plays. A painted background showing houses would be in place throughout his last two surviving dramas, *Women at the Assembly* and *Plutus*, but is in no way necessary.

2. Was the wearing of the phallus and padding universal?

First a distinction must be drawn between actors and the chorus. Neither the text of the plays nor the very slight evidence of art gives any reason for supposing that the chorusmen were padded or equipped with phalli. In a majority of Aristophanes' plays, including the early *Clouds*, *Wasps* and *Birds*, such appendages were quite unsuitable. It is true that the choruses of the satyr-plays which followed tragedies wore coloured loin-cloths supporting an erect phallus and a horse's tail; but that was a distinct form of drama.

The evidence of statuettes from the first half of the fourth century shows that many comic actors then, and perhaps all who played male slaves, wore a phallus. Aristophanes' text proves it for the old man Philokleon in *Wasps* and for Euripides' kinsman in *Women at the Thesmophoria*. The latter when detected in his disguise as a woman and stripped tries in a hilarious scene to hide the evidence of masculinity by pushing it backwards and forwards between his legs. The same actor might play more than one part in a play. If he had at some point to represent a woman, the phallus would be concealed by her long dress. Some male characters may have worn a long tunic that provided cover. The effeminate Agathon in *Women at the Thesmophoria* certainly had none that could be seen, and the absence of a penis may have been made visible to the spectators as well as remarked on by the kinsman of Euripides.

It has been argued that in *Clouds* Aristophanes attempted to get rid of this feature. In the parabasis the chorus says that the play has not come 'having sewn on a piece of dangling leather, red at the end, and thick, to make the children laugh'. That may mean no phalli (and if so, the characters' tunics cannot have been abbreviated); but it may be no more than a disclaimer of exaggerated caricature; it may also mean that the actors wore them tied up, a fashion to be seen in some artistic representations.

There are scenes where characters are beaten, notably one in *Frogs*, where Dionysus and his slave Xanthias are stripped to stage nakedness, that is to tights and phalli, and whipped to establish which is the god, for he will not feel pain. Padding would allow this to be done more realistically. But the starving Megarian of *The Acharnians*, although he might have a distended belly, could not be appropriately padded elsewhere. The fourth-century statuettes show that then at least not all actors were padded and it is plausible to suppose that Aristophanes' plays too had thin men as well as fat.

3. *Had the stage-building three doors or one?*

No tragedy suggests the use of more than central double-doors, and comedy was played in the same theatre. But when it was reconstructed by Lycurgus between 338 and 330 B C, three doorways were certainly provided, of which normally two and sometimes three were required by plays of that time. It is a matter of dispute whether more than one was already used by Aristophanes.

It would be possible to produce all his plays with only one door. The audience would accept it as a convention that the single stage-door was successively the entrance to different houses. Yet perhaps imagination would be strained in that scene of *The Acharnians* (1097–1110, 1118–25) where the same door would have to serve over and over again in successive lines for that of Dikaiopolis and that of Lamachus. There are other plays where, if only one door was available, the dramatist seems to create unnecessary difficulties, notably a scene in *Clouds*. Pheidippides refuses to become a pupil in Socrates' school and retires into his own house. Strepsiades declares that he must do what his son will not do and join the school himself. He immediately knocks upon the door of the 'thinking-shop'. Is that the same door through which Pheidippides had gone only seven lines previously? He had to be removed from the stage, but if there was only one door, why did he not go off to the side, as if going to the town? Probability seems to me to be in favour of three doors. The stage-building was constructed for use in comedy as well as tragedy and there was no reason why tragedy should employ the side-doors that were needed for comedy.[1]

4. *Were there women in the audience?*

Some women certainly attended tragedies in the early fourth century. Were they also to be seen at comedies in the late fifth? One passage strongly suggests that they were, Aristophanes *Peace* 962–7:

> *Trygaios.* And throw some barley to the spectators.
> *Servant.* There! Done!
> *Trygaios.* You've given it them already?
> *Servant.* Yes, by Hermes. Of all the spectators here there's not one who hasn't got a barley-grain.
> *Trygaios.* The *women* didn't get any.
> *Servant.* No, but the men will give them some tonight.

The clue to these exchanges is that the word for barley (*krithe*) was also slang for penis. To build on a joke is dangerous, but this one loses point unless there were some women among the audience.

The passage has been interpreted to show that the women sat at the back, where grain scattered by the actor would not reach them. That is a humourless conclusion. The servant who cries 'There! Done!' so rapidly will not have made more than a single empty-handed gesture; so far as that goes, the women may have sat with their menfolk. Nevertheless it may be true that they did sit at the back. In any case it is not likely that they were very numerous. The festival may have been an occasion for leaving their

[1] Cf. K. J. Dover, The Skene in Aristophanes, *Proceedings of the Cambridge Philological Society*, 1966, pp. 2–17.

THE COMIC THEATRE OF GREECE AND ROME

houses, but probably few husbands would encourage their wives to come to comedies or be willing to pay for their tickets. Many women would have no interest in the political allusions or knowledge of the persons attacked. It is hard to say whether they would have been bored or shocked by the numerous indecencies or whether they would have enjoyed them more if they sat together and apart. Aristophanes obviously wrote for a male audience; nothing is addressed to women. But that does not mean that women were excluded from the theatre. Nor can their absence from performances of New Comedy safely be deduced from the fact that Menander ended three plays by calling on men and boys for their applause; women may have been too few to earn a mention, or decorum may have required them to refrain from noisy approval. Slaves provide a problem of similar uncertainty. Presumably a ticket would get them in; but there would be few of them.

5. *Were any masks portrait-masks?*

The question arises with regard to Lamachus and Euripides in *The Acharnians*, to Socrates in *Clouds*, to others elsewhere. When living persons were introduced as characters in comedy was an attempt made to reproduce or caricature their features? Aristophanes explicitly says that the Paphlagonian in his *Knights*, who stands for Cleon, does not wear a mask that is like him. He gives as a reason that the real face was so frightful that the mask-maker could not stand trying to imitate it. It would be unwise to use a joke of this kind as a basis for generalising about the use of portrait-masks.

Clearly if a mask represented some living man's face, it must have been by way of caricature. The mask-maker would exaggerate features that were in any way striking, Pericles' high skull or Socrates' snub nose. It is by such exaggerations that the modern cartoonist at once distorts his subjects and also makes them recognisable. The difficulty of making a mask that would be, not a portrait, but a symbol of a real man can be overstressed. On the other hand it must not be underestimated. Some men's faces are so ordinary that they do not lend themselves to caricature. Perhaps Cleon's was such a one.

156

Glossary

anapaest: two short syllables followed by a long; see *metre*.

antepirrhema: a section of the parabasis (q.v.) symmetrically corresponding to the epirrhema (q.v.).

antode: a section of the parabasis (q.v.) symmetrically corresponding to the ode (q.v.).

bacchiac: a short syllable followed by two long; see *metre*.

choregos: lit. 'chorus-leader', not its leader and spokesman on the stage (koryphaios), but the man responsible for its costumes and training.

cretic: two long syllables enclosing one short; see *metre*.

deme: one of the administrative groups into which the Athenians were divided, for the most part territorially based but with hereditary membership. 2. The local centre of the group; in the country 'village'.

dimeter: a verse consisting of two metrical units; see *metre*.

dithyramb: a choral song of religious origin, but developed as a display of musical talent.

epirrhema: a section of the parabasis (q.v.), consisting of sixteen or twenty trochaic tetrameters.

hetaira: courtesan, lit. 'female companion'. The term covers a wide variety of women, slave and free; all that they have in common is that their relations with their 'lovers' are expected to be temporary.

iambus: a short syllable followed by a long; see *metre*.

liturgy: a public service required of the richer citizens in turn; at Athens the most onerous were the equipment, maintenance, and command of a naval vessel for a year and the dressing and training of a chorus to compete at a public festival.

metre: ancient metres were based on a division of syllables into long (or heavy) and short (or light). In Greek and in classical Latin prosody the former comprise all which contain a long vowel or a diphthong or which end with a consonant that precedes another in the same or the following word. They are indicated by a horizontal line (—) and the short syllables, all others, are indicated by ◡.

THE COMIC THEATRE OF GREECE AND ROME

Some metres, including most of those used in comedy, are named after the feet which characterise them: *iambic* ($\cup$ —), *trochaic* (— $\cup$), *cretic* (— $\cup$ —), *bacchiac* ($\cup$ — —), and *anapaestic* ($\cup \cup$ —). But the unit was not the foot, but what is called the *metron*. The iambic metron was $\asymp$ — $\cup$ —, where $\asymp$ indicates that either a long or a short syllable is allowable; three of these metra constitute the iambic *trimeter*, always the metre of comedy's opening scenes. Subject to various restrictions, two short syllables may be substituted for a long. The trochaic metron was — $\cup$ — $\asymp$, usually grouped in fours, the final syllable of the last being suppressed; these make the trochaic *tetrameter*, which I have often called 'long trochaics'.

The Roman dramatists took over these metres, but with modifications: a syllable ending with a consonant was not necessarily long, and *spondees* (— —) often replace iambic or trochaic feet. The reason for these changes is disputed, but much of their scansion can be plausibly explained by the fact that Latin words, like those of English but unlike those of classical Greek, had a stress accent, which affected the length or weight of unaccented syllables. The dramatists scanned by ear, not by Greek rules.

ode: a choral song which was a standard element in the parabasis (q.v.).

orchestra: dancing-floor, circular in the Greek theatre, semicircular in the Roman, where it was used for seating.

parabasis: a section of fifth-century comedies in which the action was suspended and the chorus addressed the audience.

parasite: one who earned his meals by making himself agreeable, whether as a flatterer or a butt or a tool, to his patron.

parodoi: passages leading into the orchestra or to the stage past the ends of the semicircular or horseshoe-shaped auditorium.

phlyakes: comic actors of southern Italy.

satyr: mythological attendant of Dionysus, represented on the stage by a man naked except for a loin-cloth to which were attached an erect phallus and a horse's tail.

senarius: 'six-footer', the Latin equivalent of the Greek trimeter.

skene: stage-building, lit. 'tent'. A tent will have served as background and dressing room for early players.

tetrameter: a verse consisting of four metrical units; see *metre*.

trimeter: a verse consisting of three metrical units; see *metre*.

trochee: a long syllable followed by a short; see *metre*.

Select Bibliography

So far as modern scholarship is concerned, this list is very selective and confined to books in the English language.

1. ARISTOPHANES

(a) Surviving plays

The Acharnians 425 BC	*Lysistrata* 411 BC
Knights 424 BC	*Thesmophoriazusae* 411 BC
Clouds 423 BC	(*Women at the Thesmophoria*)
Wasps 422 BC	*Frogs* 405 BC
Peace 421 BC	*Ecclesiazusae* 392 BC
Birds 414 BC	(*Women at the Assembly*)
	Plutus (*Wealth*) 388 BC

(b) Texts and translations

Best complete text, not always satisfactory: V. Coulon in Budé series (Paris, 1928–30) with French translation by H. van Daele. Only complete English commentary: B. B. Rogers (Bell, London, 1902–15); his text and neat decorous verse translation used in Loeb series. Several plays edited with commentary in a Clarendon Press series: *Clouds* (1965) by K. J. Dover, *Ecclesiazuase* (1973) by R. G. Ussher, *Peace* (1964) by M. Platnauer, *Wasps* (1970) by D. MacDowell; others are expected. Other useful editions: *The Acharnians* by W. J. M. Starkie (London, Macmillan, 1909); *Birds* by W. W. Merry (Oxford University Press, edn. 3, 1896), *Frogs* by W. B. Stanford (London, Macmillan, 1963), *Knights* by R. A. Neil (Cambridge University Press, 1901).

Some modern versions are far removed from the original text: being conceived as adaptations suitable for our stage. Readable and more reliable in detail are two Penguin volumes in prose, *Wasps, Thesmophoriazusae*, and *Frogs* by D. Barrett (1964) and *The Acharnians, Clouds* and *Lysistrata* by A. H. Sommerstein (1973).

(c) General

K. J. Dover, *Aristophanic Comedy* (London, Batsford, 1972): up-to-date, individual, wide-ranging; has a useful short bibliography.

C. W. Dearden, *The Stage of Aristophanes* (London, Athlone Press, 1976).

G. Murray, *Aristophanes* (Oxford, Clarendon Press, 1933) has enthusiasm which compensates for some untenable views. The most recent treatment of Aristophanes' political views is in G. E. M. de Ste Croix, *The Origin of the Peloponnesian War* (London, Duckworth, 1972), appendix xxix, pp. 355–76, where references will be found to earlier work.

2. MENANDER

(a) Plays of which more than 100 lines survive in a fair state of preservation

Aspis (*The Shield*)	*Misumenos* (*Hated*)
Georgos (*The Farmer*)	*Perikeiromene* (*Shorn Tresses*)
Dis Exapaton (*A Double Deceit*)	*Samia* (*A Woman from Samos*)
Dyskolos (*The Curmudgeon*)	*Sikyonios* or *Sikyonioi*
Epitrepontes (*The Arbitrants*)	(*The Man* [or *The Men*] *from*
Kolax (*The Flatterer*)	*Sikyon*)

Only *Dyskolos*, apparently the earliest, can be dated (317 BC); *Epitrepontes* and *Misumenos* seem to be late.

(b) Texts and translations

Text: F. H. Sandbach in Oxford Classical Texts (1972). Commentary: A. W. Gomme and F. H. Sandbach, *Menander* (Oxford, Clarendon Press, 1973); E. W. Handley, *The Dyskolos of Menander* (London, Methuen, 1965).

Menander still awaits his translator. E. G. Turner, *The Samian Woman* (London, Athlone Press, 1972) is a good version of that play. The most accessible translation of *Dyskolos* is by P. H. Vellacott (London, OUP, 1960), reprinted in Penguin Classics (1973) along with remains of seven other plays which are often unreliably presented. More faithful versions of *Epitrepontes* and *Perikeiromene* are to be found in L. A. Post, *Menander, Three Plays* (London, Routledge, and New York, Dutton, 1929).

(c) General

T. B. L. Webster, *An Introduction to Menander* (Manchester University Press, 1974).

3. OTHER GREEK COMEDY

(a) Texts and translations

T. Kock, *Comicorum Atticorum Fragmenta* (Leipzig, Teubner, 3 vols, 1880–8).

SELECT BIBLIOGRAPHY

G. Kaibel, *Comicorum Graecorum Fragmenta*, vol. I.1 (all published, Berlin, Weidmann, 1899): dramatists of Southern Italy and Sicily.

C. Austin, *Comicorum Graecorum Fragmenta in Papyris Reperta* (Berlin and New York, de Gruyter, 1973) purposely omits most of Menander.

J. M. Edmonds, *The Fragments of Attic Comedy* (Leiden, Brill, 3 vols, 1957–61) has an English verse translation of a very unreliable text.

(b) General

T. B. L. Webster, *Studies in Later Greek Comedy* (Manchester University Press, edn. 2, 1970).

O. E. Legrand, translated by J. Loeb, *The New Greek Comedy* (London, Heinemann, and New York, Putnam's Sons, 1917). The original French volume is entitled *Daos* (Paris, 1910).

G. Norwood, *Greek Comedy* (London, Methuen, 1931), useful for information on early authors other than Aristophanes.

4. PLAUTUS

(a) Surviving plays

In the first century B C the Roman scholar Varro listed twenty-one plays universally agreed to be by Plautus, and they can be presumed identical with the twenty-one we have. The following list gives the titles by which they now go and the author and title of the Greek original if known. A title not translated is a proper name.

Asinaria (*The Donkeys*) Demophilus, *Onagos*
Aulularia (*The Little Jar*) ? Menander
Amphitruo
Bacchides (*The Bacchis Sisters*) Menander, *Dis Exapaton*
Captivi (*The Prisoners*)
Casina Diphilus, *Klerumenoi*
Cistellaria (*A Little Box*) Menander, *Synaristosai*
Curculio
Epidicus
Menaechmi (*The Menaechmus Twins*)
Mercator (*The Merchant*) Philemon, *Emporos*
Miles Gloriosus (*The Boastful Soldier*)
Mostellaria (*The Ghost*) ? Philemon, *Phasma*
Persa (*The Persian*)
Poenulus (*The Little Carthaginian*) ? Alexis, *Karchedonios*
Pseudolus
Rudens (*The Rope*) Diphilus

Stichus Menander, *Adelphoe A*

Trinummus (*Three Pieces of Silver*) Philemon, *Thesauros*

Truculentus

Vidularia (*The Travelling Bag*), much mutilated.

Asinaria, Cistellaria, Mercator, and *Miles Gloriosus* are probably earlier than *Stichus* (200 BC). There is some reason for dating the rest between 194 and 184: *Pseudolus* belongs to 191 and *Casina* is later than 186.

(b) Texts and translations

Text: W. M. Lindsay in Oxford Classical Texts (2 vols, 1904–5); F. Leo (Berlin, Weidmann, 2 vols, 1895–6).

Translations: P. Nixon in the Loeb series; E. F. Watling in Penguin classics; G. E. Duckworth, *The Complete Roman Drama* (New York, Random House, 1942).

(c) General

E. Segal, *Roman Laughter* (Harvard University Press, 1968). See also below, under 'The Roman Theatre'.

5. TERENCE

(a) Plays

Andria (*A Woman from Andros*) 166 BC Menander

Hecyra (*The Mother-in-law*) 165 and 160 BC Apollodorus

Heautontimorumenos 163 BC Menander

(*The Man Who Punished Himself*)

Eunuchus (*The Eunuch*) 161 BC Menander

Phormio 161 BC Apollodorus, *Epidikazomenos*

Adelphoe (*The Brothers*) 160 BC Menander

These dates are probable rather than certain.

(b) Texts and translations

Text: R. Kauer and W. M. Lindsay in Oxford Classical Texts (1926). With commentary, G. P. Shipp, *Andria* (Melbourne, OUP, edn. 2, 1960); R. H. Martin, *Phormio* (London, Methuen, 1959) and *Adelphoe* (Cambridge University Press, 1976). Translations: J. Sargeaunt in the Loeb series; P. Borie, C. Carrier, and D. Parker, *The Complete Comedies of Terence* (New Brunswick, Rutgers University Press, 1974).

(c) General

G. Norwood, *The Art of Terence* (Oxford, Blackwell, 1923), may stimulate dissent and thought.

SELECT BIBLIOGRAPHY

6. GENERAL

(a) Festivals, Theatres, and Performance

H. C. Baldry, *The Greek Tragic Theatre* (London, Chatto and Windus, 1971) gives an excellent short account of the theatre in fifth-century Athens. Fuller and more specialised books include the following:

P. D. Arnott, *Greek Scenic Conventions in the Fifth Century BC* (Oxford University Press, 1962).

M. Bieber, *The History of the Greek and Roman Theatre* (Princeton University Press, edn. 2, 1961), lavishly illustrated, dogmatic text, good bibliography.

A. W. Pickard-Cambridge, *The Theatre of Dionysus in Athens* (Oxford, Clarendon Press, 1946), standard work on the buildings. A. W. Pickard-Cambridge, *The Dramatic Festivals of Athens* (Oxford, Clarendon Press, edn. 2 revised by J. Gould and D. M. Lewis, 1968), an outstanding work with extensive bibliography, but often needs a knowledge of Greek.

G. M. Sifakis, *Parabasis and Animal Choruses* (London, Athlone Press, 1971).

A. D. Trendall and T. B. L. Webster, *Illustrations of Greek Drama* (London, Phaidon Press, 1971).

T. B. L. Webster, *Greek Theatre Production* (London, Methuen, edn. 2, 1970).

(b) Origins of Comedy

A. W. Pickard-Cambridge, *Dithyramb, Tragedy and Comedy* (Oxford, Clarendon Press, edn. 2 revised by T. B. L. Webster, 1962).

(c) The Roman Theatre

W. Beare, *The Roman Stage* (London, Methuen, edn. 3 revised, 1969), wide-ranging and mostly convincing, but not on the 'Law of Five Acts'. Short bibliography.

M. Bieber, see above.

G. E. Duckworth, *The Nature of Roman Comedy* (Princeton University Press, 1952) thorough and sensible, has an informative chapter about influence on later literature down to twentieth century. Extensive bibliography.

(d) New Comedy

W. G. Arnott, *Menander, Plautus, Terence* (Oxford, Clarendon Press, 1975), an up-to-date survey with much bibliographical material.

INDEX

INDEX

Bucco, 105
buffoon, 43
Byzantine scholars, 9, 10

(Statius) Caecilius, 135, 137–8, 147
(C. Iulius) Caesar, 116, 147
Callistratus, 18
cantica, 120–2, 134
censorship, 56
characterisation, 63, 77, 82–4, 99–100, 130, 133–4, 137, 144
chorēgos, 12, 23, 24, 71, 157
chorus, 12, 15, 42, 79; cost, 12; costume, 20, 54; dancing, 25; decay of, 57; song, 22–3, 25, 43, 44, 57
chorus-leader (*koryphaios*), 22, 25
Chrēmonidēs, 68
Christianity, 150
(M. Tullius) Cicero, 109, 110, 111, 115, 116, 120, 121, 149
Claudius, emperor, 75
Cleōn, 19, 21, 27, 45, 58, 156
Cleōnymus, 45
(P.) Clōdius (Pulcher), 116
Cloudcuckooland, 27
comedies, number of at Dionysia, 12, 73; at Lēnaia, 12
comedy, derivation of the word, 53; origins, 51–4
competition, 11–12, 71, 73–4, 117
contractors, 18, 71
cooks, 60, 82, 92–3
Coriannō, 50–1
costume, *see* actors *and* chorus
courtesans, 51, 59, 83
Cratinus, 24, 41, 42, 45; *Cheirōnes*, 50; *Dionysalexandros*, 49; *Pytinē*, 41
curtain, 114–15

Dāos, 63
Dark Ages of Greece, 9
Dekker, *Shoemaker's Holiday*, 139

deikeliktai, 53, 106
Delphi, 11, 74, 79
Dēlos, 52, 74
dēmarch, 71
Dēmeās, 63
Dēmētrius, Besieger of Cities, 57, 68
Dēmētrius of Phalērum, 76
Dēmophilus, 119
Dikaiopolis, 19–24, 58
Dioclētian, 75
Diodōrus, 71
Diomēdēs, 111–12
Diōn of Prusa, 74
Dionysia, City, 11, 12, 13, 17, 18, 26–8, 71; rural, 20
Dionysus, loved patron of comedy, 11, 16, 18, 41, 47, 53, 74, 106, 109; ridiculous character in comedy, 32, 46, 48–9, 60, 139; see *also* Dionysia *and* Artists of Dionysus
Diphilus, 67, 73, 76, 80, 119, 140; *Klērūmenoi*, 126, 127
dithyrambs, 13, 53
Dōnātus, 112, 139, 142, 145, 146, 149
Dossennus, 105

educator, poet as, 22, 30, 101, 117, 150
Egypt, 10, 41
ekkyklēma, 21
Eleusis, 71
(Q.) Ennius, 121, 139
entrance-fees, 18
Ephesus, 74
Epicharmus, 51–3
Epidaurus, 71
equitēs, 109
Erōs, 85
Etruscans, 103–4
Eupolis, 24, 41, 42, 43, 44, 45, 53; *Demes*, 44; *Marikās*, 42

165

INDEX

Menander—*cont.*
82, 83, 85, 86, 87–100; *Sikyō-
nios*, 79, 83, 87; *Synāristōsai*, 86;
Theophorūmenē, 74
Meres, Francis, 151
metre, 20, 21, 22, 43, 47, 77, 106,
119–20, 152, 157–8
mimes, 115, 116–17, 149
monologues, 18–19, 21, 65–6, 87–8,
90–1, 98, 127, 128–30, 141, 146
Montaigne, 151
Moschiōn, 63, 64
mythology, burlesqued, 49, 57,
106; Greek in Plautus, 124–5

(Cn.) Naevius, 106, 108, 139
names, invented, 123–4; stock,
63; unusual, 64
Naples, 103
Nōvius, 105

Orange, 108
orchēstra, 16 f., 18, 108, 158
Orchomenos, 74
origins of comedy, 51–4
Oscan, 104, 125
Othō, 109

padding, 18, 55, 154
Panathēnaia, 11
Pappus, 105
papyrus, 10
parabasis, 22, 24, 32, 42, 57, 158
parasites, 59, 61, 158
parodoi, 16, 18, 72, 158
parody, 20, 21, 24, 28, 33, 38,
47–8, 59
Peisthetairos, 27, 43
(T. Publilius) Polliō, 110
Peloponnesian War, 15, 34–7
Pericles, 21, 45, 49, 50
personal attacks, 19, 23, 37–40,
44–5, 49–50, 52, 54, 56, 59, 74,
116
Peter Pan, 65

phallic songs, 51–2
phallus, 18, 20, 52, 53, 55, 153–4
Pherecratēs, *Coriannō*, 50
Philippidēs, 56
Philēmōn, 67, 76, 77, 119, 161,
162
phlyākes, 106, 158
Phrynichus, 42
piper, 15, 20, 54, 79, 114, 137
Pio, G. B., 113
place, free shift of, 20, 21, 23, 27,
28, 32, 35, 153; unity maintained, 29, 57
Plato, 24, 59; *Symposium*, 13
Plautus, 10, 78, 104, 108, 113–14,
118–34, 137, 139, 140, 147,
151–2, 161–2; *Amphitruō*, 112,
151; *Asināria*, 110, *Bacchidēs*,
86, 113, 123, 126, 127, 128–33;
Casina, 120, 127; *Cistellāria*, 86,
110; *Curculiō*, 114; *Epidicus*,
110, 127; *Menaechmi*, 112, 151;
Mercātor, 126; *Miles Glōriōsus*,
151; *Persa*, 61; *Poenulus*, 109,
126; *Pseudolus*, 114, 149; *Stichus*,
87, 107, 110; *Vidulāria*, 119
plot, 57–8, 77–8, 87, 126, 152;
truncation of, 126–7
Plutarch, 74, 85, 101
pnigos, 43
politics, 21, 27, 28, 43–4, 56, 67–9
(Iulius) Pollux, 64, 72
Pompey (Cn. Pompeius Magnus),
108
(L.) Pompōnius, 105
prizes, 11, 13, 71
prologues, 65–7, 81, 135–6, 138–9,
141
Pseudartabās, 19
Publilius Syrus, 117
puns, 20, 23, 137

Quintilian (M. Fabius Quinti-
liānus), 110, 149

167

revivals, 73, 116, 127, 136, 149, 151
Rhinthōn, 106
(P.) Roscius (Gallus), 110, 112, 121
running slave, 125–6

St Paul's School, London, 151
Samos, 24
sausage-seller, 28, 43
Santra, 136
scene-painting, 72–3, 153
(P. Cornēlius) Scipio, 136
seating, 16, 108–9, 155
Sēmus of Dēlos, 52
(L. Annaeus) Seneca, 115
senators, 108
Shakespeare, 113; Comedy of Errors, 112, 151; Winter's Tale, 78
Sheridan, 65
Sicily, 51, 60
Sicyōn, 53
skēnē, 17–18, 72, 108, 153, 154–5
slaves as characters in plays, 19, 20, 21, 28, 55, 60–1, 62, 64, 69, 81, 88, 96–7, 115, 125, 143, 154, 155; in Menander, 84, 100; in Plautus, 125–7; actors at Rome, 109–10; manumitted writers of comedy, 117, 135; spectators, 109, 156
Smikrinēs, 64
soldiers, 59, 82–3
Sōcratēs, 9, 13, 27, 44
song, by chorus, 22–3, 43, 44, 57; by actor, 24, 120–1, 127, 137
Sophoclēs, 71; Electra, 67
Sparta, 19, 20, 53, 106
stage, 16, 72, 105, 108
stage-building, see skēnē
stock characters, 45–6, 61–3
stock motifs, 45–6, 61–3
Stratoclēs, 56
(L. Cornēlius) Sulla, 73, 110

symmetry, 20, 22, 43, 98
Syracuse, 51, 53, 67, 103
Syros, 63

Tarentum, 103, 106
Terence (P. Terentius Afer), 10, 62, 78, 112, 113, 135–47, 149–52, 162; Adelphoe, 85, 135, 136, 139–42, 145–6; Andria, 139, 142, 151; Eunūchus, 82, 83, 139, 142–4, 146, 151; Heautontimorūmenos, 83; Hecyra, 73, 136; Phormiō, 73, 151
Terentius Lūcānus, 135
theatre at Acharnae, 71; at Athens, 16–8, 72 (plan, 16); at Delphi, 74; at Eleusis, 71; at Epidaurus, 71; at Ephesus, 74; at Orange, 108; at Orchomenos, 74; at Peiraeus, 71; at Rome, 108 (plan, 17); at Samos, 74; at Thebēs, 74
Thebes, 53, 74
Theognis, 19
theoric fund, 18, 69
time, elastic treatment of, 20, 22, 37, 27
tragedies, 12, 13; influence of, 58, 67, 86

Udall, Ralph Roister Doister, 151

(M. Terentius) Varro, 111–12
Virgil, 125, 138

war, Aristophanes' attitude to, 33–7
wedding-party, 27, 35, 60, 90, 98
Westminster School, 151
Wolsey, Cardinal, 151
women in audience, 109, 155–6; in plays, 37, 50, 56, 83, 86
Words, Greek in Plautus, 124; play on 122–3; see also puns